Shoulders I've Rubbed

(The Extraordinary Story of an Ordinary Bloke)

by Malcolm Lenny

Published 2017

ISBN-13: 978-1547186600
ISBN-10: 1547186607

Dedication

To my wife Maureen, my 3 daughters Jane, Karen and Sue, my step-son Adam and all of my 10 Grandchildren. Thanks for all your years of support throughout good and not-so-good times.

It couldn't always have been fun when you were told, "Hurry up and finish your tea. We've got to go and see Dad or Granddad play".

Also, thanks to all my friends and colleagues in the Television Industry for still being my friends.

Lastly, thanks to all the musicians that I've played with over the last 60 years.

"It's been Great!"

Foreword

I first knew Malcolm in the 1950s where we both lived and went to school in Balham, South London and here we are nearly 70 years later!

After a brief foray into skiffle (didn't everybody?) Malcolm spent five years as a professional musician, touring, making records (with Joe Meek) with his band The Packabeats. They performed on radio and television shows in the U.K. and Europe.

His second band The Hi-Fi's went to Germany and The Star Club in Hamburg was a regular gig and he is still in contact with friends he made in Germany

He finished playing professionally in 1967 when his first daughter was born (two more followed!) and decided to get a 'proper' job.

The next 35 years was spent working for various television companies, initially London Weekend Television. During this time he met many TV stars and personalities who you will read about in this book.

He retired at 62 and worked part-time in a local music

shop. A regular visitor was Tony Green, a great country singer with whom he still performs in a band called Side by Side at the ripe old age of 75! (I'm the bass player for my sins!)

Enjoy this book, I'm sure you will!

Pete Mills.

Introduction

After being told that I should make a note of all the stories and people I've met during my life in music, as well as working in the television industry for 34 years, I felt compelled to put my own reminisces down on paper. It's just that it occurred to me that I've met an awful lot of quite well-known people during my life, albeit some in only a small way.

I played in '60s pop groups The Packabeats and recorded 3 singles with Joe Meek (The TELSTAR Man) and The Hi-Fi's and recorded two singles with Glyn Johns (The Beatles record producer after George Martin). I also had a No.1 & No.4 in the German charts in '65 and '66 and a hit album with The Hi-Fi's.

Later on I worked in the TV industry, mostly with London Weekend Television (ITV) and later SKY TV (Satellite TV).

It's been a very interesting and fun journey.

Malcolm Lenny

--CONTENTS--

Chapter 1   Beginnings

Me aged one year

My story begins mid-second World War time. Born April 30th 1942. Son of Arthur Ernest Lenny, a Westminster born, kitchen catering equipment salesman and a Mum born in Aldershot, of a military Father. As we lived in Balham South London, Mum, Gladys May Lenny, was given the dubious title of, "A Battersea Mother", although, strictly speaking, we lived in the Borough of Wandsworth and we were fiercely protective of that fact. That was when she was shipped off to Shepton Mallett in Somerset to produce me. After all, Balham was not a good place to have a baby as Mr A. Hitler had designs on reducing London to a pile of rubble.

I was always told that I was born in a stately home owned by a Lord Padget called Cranmore Hall. My Balham friends were always envious of that. Apparently the Luftwaffe bombed the city of Bath the day after I was born so I got the notion that Hitler was out to get me.

A few days after I had "arrived", Mum and I were moved up to her cousin's place in Preston and guess what? The Luftwaffe bombed Preston Docks! Anyway it went a bit quiet after that for a very short while so Dad, Arthur, said it was all right to come back to London. Dad was in the ARP - that's Air Raid Precautions to the uninitiated. He was too young for the First World War and too old for the second. Anyway, he had lousy feet, which he kindly passed on to me! My sister Barbara had stayed with him, as she was six and a half years older than me and therefore able to handle the German invasion.

Dad used to ride his bike around the streets of Balham, fire watching, when the incendiary bombs were dropping. Our cat Mickey used to accompany him on his rounds. He once told the amazing story about an eccentric gentleman who lived in the next street who thought he was General Montgomery. That is, he dressed in khaki shirt and trousers, leather waistcoat, black beret and he carried a swagger stick under his arm at all times. The story goes that in the middle of an air raid, Dad was passing "The Field Marshall's" house when the front, upstairs window was thrown up and he shouted, "I say old boy, there's one of those damned things on my bed!". Dad threw his bike in the kerb, ran upstairs and, sure enough, there was an incendiary canister fizzing and popping in the middle of the bed. He picked up the mattress, bedclothes and all and threw them out of the window into the road. The Field Marshall's answer to that was "Now where the hell am I going to sleep, you bloody fool!" Some people are just never grateful for anything.

So with The Battle of Britain over and won, Mum and little me came back to London and then Mr Hitler started his V1 Doodlebug business. This was '43/'44 I think and I know it's supposed to be impossible to remember anything at a very young age but I swear I can remember the "drumming" sound of a "doodlebug" engine.

On one occasion, I have a vivid memory of a V1 engine conking out and being grabbed from my cot wrapped in a blanket and seeing people running to the air-raid shelter in the street outside our house. Impossible? Maybe.

When the war ended, I was two and a half. Most of the country had Victory street parties and Gosberton Road, Balham, S.W.12, was no exception. I can remember trestle tables and flags and red, white and blue bunting everywhere. The old bomb shelters were every 50 yards up every road but we had plenty of room in between. At the top end of the road there was an empty piece of land, probably a bombed site where people had lived, where the local neighbours had erected a large gallows where they hanged a stuffed dummy of Adolf Hitler. I had nightmares about that figure for years after the war. Only after a fair bit of time did I realise that the piece of land at the top of the road corresponded with another, three houses down the road from us at number 84 and another at the bottom end opposite the Post office. Dad told me that a "stick" of bombs had dropped in our street while we were all in the cellar! We used to play in our gang on the bombed sites after the war, not knowing that people had been killed there.

About two miles from us was Clapham Common. It was a large piece of common land for the locals to use for recreation. A Lancaster Bomber had made a forced landing there after a raid over Germany and it had stayed there until the war was over. I remember being taken on board and shown all the ins and outs of that wonderful aeroplane. I was about six but I remember it well.

My Infants/Primary School, Hearnville Road, didn't open until I was nearly six. That kind of explains my late development. It was chalk, slates and a break every so often to go out into the playground to shake our dusters. After two years we moved up to the Juniors and we got to learn how to do real "joined-up writing". How the hell we managed that with pens that had nibs resembling arrowheads I'll never know.

As people frequently tell you, our teachers were all ladies of a certain age with ample bosoms and moustaches. Well it's true. Our Head Mistress was a formidable lady named Miss Edith B. Cox who squeaked as she walked and she pounded the piano into submission at assembly every morning. She terrified us when she was angry, mainly because she went so red in the face we all thought she would explode! She had an office, off the school hall, up a long, single, open staircase, with the staff room directly opposite. It was always scary to climb those stairs because you always felt you were in some kind of trouble even if you weren't.

Hearnville School had had its own motto, contrived by Miss Cox that said:

"DO RIGHT, BECAUSE IT IS RIGHT."

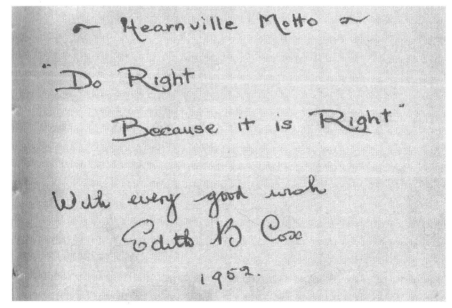

Hearnville School Motto

I still have that motto, written in her own fair hand in my autograph book because that's the kind of thing you did then.

Miss Cox was a tough old bird but somehow I thought we loved her in a strange way. She made the school celebrate Empire Day in full costumes complete with Maypole dancing and Morris dancing. I remember poor old Charlie Stroud getting the cane on his hands all because he cocked up the pattern on the Maypole. I had my knuckles rapped but that was my partner Robert Hunter, in the Morris dancing doing his best to hit me as I was trying to hit him.

 Christmas was always a great time because we had the world's best carol concert in the hall and whoever got to play Good King Wenceslas got to sing from the balcony outside Miss Cox's office. I never made it to King or his Page, but I was the "Peasant, gathering winter fuel" one year.

Every class would put on a play connected to Christmas. Not Nativity plays but comedies. Great fun. But above all I loved the open fires in the hall and every classroom. The gas lighting added subdued lighting and extra warmth too. We all had girlfriends too, if we were lucky. I must have

Empire Day Maypole Dancing

been extra lucky because at 11, I had two! Both called Christine: one Gatfield, the other Bartlett. If those ladies ever get to read this, I'd like them to know that I loved them both. Well, if it's possible to be in love at 11!

I remember coming home from school one day to find a mobile crane with a massive metal ball on a chain, knocking down the old air-raid shelters in our road. That was when it was discovered that the whole front of our house was loose! Consequently we had to spend a few weeks with no front on the house and only a tarpaulin keeping out the weather and any predators who happened to be passing. Still, we didn't have two pennies to rub together so it didn't matter anyway.

Sometimes Mum would send me to school with two thicknesses of cardboard from a Kellogg's Corn Flakes packet to cover the hole in the sole of my sandals. That would last one day, every day, until Dad had enough money to buy me another pair. Dad even cut the front out of the sandals so my toes could stick out over the end. That's probably why I've got such awful feet now. Hammered toes, the lot. Those times were tough but we were all in the same boat and England was recovering from the cost of the war. It's often been said that it never did us any harm but it certainly made me appreciate things in later life.

A holiday in those days meant a week in a caravan at Sheerness on the Isle of Sheppey. Or a Bed & Breakfast at Broadstairs. Soon after that the "holiday camps" began and Dad took us to one at Leysdown-on-Sea also on Sheppey. We had a great time and our family struck up friendships with some families from Gosport, Hampshire. I'm very pleased to say that I'm still friends with one of the sons of a family and I was about 12 when he was born.

In those days, everyone took the 11+ exam. I didn't earn
enough marks to get me to Battersea Grammar School,
where all the clever boys went, but I had the chance at,
what was called a Governor's Place. This meant taking an
entrance test at Archbishop Tennisons School right next
door to The Oval Cricket Ground. The school smelled stale.
It was very dark and so old fashioned that the Masters
wore Mortar Board and Gown. It was like something out of
"Billy Bunter's Greyfriars School". I hated it! In the test, I
put my name and number on the top of the sheet and just
sat there with my arms folded. I didn't want to go to that
school. My Dad was furious. I'd let him down. I wanted to
go to a school where my friends were going. So I got my
way and went to Aristotle Secondary School at Clapham
North.

I was 11 when Queen Elizabeth II was crowned. Dad had
bought a 12 inch Ferguson TV set so we could all watch it.
It was a magical day, even though it rained on and off
throughout the procession. I sat the whole day in a child's
armchair meant for about a six year-old. But I was a skinny
kid so it didn't matter.

It seems a bit odd to have a Television when we always seemed so poor. At the age of 11, I was allowed to have a morning paper round. For which I received the princely sum of 11 shillings and six pence per week. I soon added an afternoon round for another four shillings and sixpence. I was out in all weathers and in the dark when it was winter. I had a bike torch on a string around my neck so I could read the numbers on the papers. Thursdays were always a nightmare because that's the day *Radio Times* and *Woman's Own* magazine came out. They made the bag twice as heavy. Sundays were just as bad because a lot of people had more than one paper.

I remember every Monday morning before I went out on my round at six thirty am, I had to light the fire under Mum's brick built "Copper". That was because Monday was washing day. Luxury!

It was so cold in our house in Winter that I had Dad's old ARP Warden's overcoat on top of my bedclothes. I felt like I was being held down by a sheet of lead because it was so heavy. My bedroom had ice <u>inside</u> the windows. There was an oil stove on the landing outside my door directly under the hatch to the loft. That was supposed to stop the pipes from freezing up. The only other heating was a coal fire in the back kitchen/dining room. Dad used to carry the hot coals on a shovel up to the front room so we could have a fire in the evening.

A lot of the last piece about my childhood must have re-kindled a lot of memories for a lot of people who grew up in similar conditions in the '40s and '50s. The *Monty Python* sketch about, "Living in a shoe box at the end of the A1, waking up at 4.00 in the morning, pushing back the lid. Getting up and licking the street clean before we went to school" etc. doesn't seem too many miles away from how it really was back then.

Chapter 2   Meeting First Celebrities

Back when the word "Teenager" had just been invented, I was about thirteen. I remember it distinctly because I had my first pair of long trousers and I was worried that I couldn't get into see football with my Dad through the turnstile marked BOYS.

Living in South London, we had a choice of teams to watch. Wimbledon, were the nearest but they were in a Minor league called The Isthmian League. That's long before they got into the proper Football league. Chelsea, were in the First Division and so were Fulham. So we had a good choice of teams to watch most Saturdays. My Dad had a friend, Ray Willis, who actually had a trial for Charlton Athletic, in South East London so although Ray didn't make it, somehow we began to go The Valley instead.

In those days, I was a real football lover and sometimes, during school holidays, I used to go with schoolmates to watch the Charlton team training. I would take my autograph book and get all my heroes to sign it. Sam Bartram was the goalkeeper and my favourite personality. Derek Ufton was Captain and played a few times for England. John Hewie was South African born and had a bit of a "dusky complexion" but somehow managed to play for Scotland! Jimmy Seed, the manager, even signed an Italian sounding player by the name of Eddie Firmani who was brilliant. He had a brother Peter, who also signed for the club. Actually the brothers were proper Londoners. I had all these guys in my first autograph book.

My second book had signatures that I collected when I went to The Schoolboys Own Exhibition at Olympia. Hands up all those who remember that? It was an annual event and, boy, did we love it! We spent all day there, without parents! It was kids heaven.

BBC TV had not been going that long and one of the first people to sign my book was the then famous in-vision TV announcer, PETER HAIG. To stand in front of the man, who appeared most days on our TV, speaking to me personally was very exciting!

Different stands had different personalities on them. One had RAY ELLINGTON. Who used to appear on *The Goon*

Show, the biggest radio comedy show of the time. Ray was so big! He played drums and sang with his quartet. Brilliant! He also used to do weird voices on the show when Spike Milligan wrote them. Ray's in my book.

The early sci-fi drama *The Quatermass Experiment* had been running on BBC Television in those days and the two actors who played the lead parts, were on the BBC stand. DON ROBINSON, who played Professor Quatermass and HUGH GRIFFITHS, who played his assistant, Leo Pugh. That programme was a milestone in TV sci-fi drama. It was real "hide behind the sofa" stuff with poor old Duncan Lamont slowly turning into a giant cactus!

Those two autographs are on the page opposite N. Ireland and Tottenham Hotspur Captain, DANNY BLANCHFLOWER. Now there was a really nice man - who everyone remembers years later when he was the surprise guest on the TV show *This Is Your Life*? Eamon Andrews said his usual, "Tonight, Danny Blanchflower, This Is Your Life". "Oh no it's not!" Said Danny and leaped over the sofa and disappeared off the stage.

On the next page is the signature of Wales and Arsenal Captain, WALLY BARNES.

Such a quiet, gentle, man but get him in his kit on a football pitch and he was a different bloke. WALLY'S signature is opposite the world famous (at the time) track cyclist, EILEEN SHERIDAN. Cycling was a big thing amongst us kids in those days but somehow I can't remember the Tour De France being known at all?

We all had push-bikes back then. Mostly they were second hand because no one could afford a new one. I had my dad's old 'heap' that weighed a ton! The chain broke one day and I came down on the cross-bar with an ear piercing scream. I still believe that's the reason why I can still sing falsetto today.

I had a brand new Phillips Kingfisher for Christmas when I was 14. I can still remember my Dad carrying it upstairs to my bedroom to pretend that Father Christmas had brought it. The thing is, Dad had been to the pub with his mates and carrying that bike when he was a little "worse for wear" was hilarious. He was gouging lumps out of the wall and scratching the banisters with every step. Mum, in a very audible 'stage' whisper was saying, "Arthur, will you be careful!" He said, "I don't care, this is for my boy" in a very slurred voice. I was under the covers trying not to let them hear me laughing. I was up at six am sitting astride my beautiful new bike, peddling backwards, with a beaming smile on my face. Some b*****d nicked it two years later when I was at Wandsworth Technical College, working my butt off to get qualifications.

Cast of The Appleyards autographs

There was a children's TV show called *The Appleyards* on at this time. It was a kind of kids soap really and we all watched it. I watched mainly because I think I was in love with one of the characters called Hazel, played by BARBARA BROWN. She was gorgeous! She was probably 15 and I was 14 but who cares? When I saw them all on the BBC stand, I had to speak to her. Of course, when I get close what happens? I can't say a word! I'm completely tongue-tied. What an idiot! Anyway, I got all of the cast's autographs.

Another children's TV show was probably the first one that taught us all about animals. This show was introduced by a gentleman called GEORGE CANSDALE. He was just like a very friendly schoolteacher. I had a nice chat with him while he was signing my book. I wish all my schoolteachers had been like Mr Cansdale.

On a BBC Sports stand, were two of my absolute sporting heroes. The great JIM LAKER, Surrey and England off-spin bowler and JIM PETERS, the brave and courageous marathon runner.

JIM LAKER still holds the record for taking 19 wickets for 90 runs! That was in 1956 in the fourth Test Match at Old Trafford against Australia. I can't see that ever happening again. It was really exciting to shake Jim's hand.

Athlete JIM PETERS will always be remembered for the time that he led the marathon right to the winning tape and collapsed yards from it. That's what I call "Rough Justice". It was an equal pleasure to shake Jim's hand.

In those days, to get up close to stars, personalities or whatever you want to call them, was a very exciting experience. I had no idea how many others I was destined to meet throughout the rest of my life.

Chapter 3   Friends

When I mentioned "Friends" in the previous chapter, I refer specifically to my three life-long mates, Bernard Thompson, Pete Mills and Dave Elliot.

Bern lived over my garden wall in the next street. Pete lived just up the road and round the corner and Dave lived up the other end of my street. Bern and I went to Aristotle School and Pete and Dave went to The Bec Shool at Tooting. We all blundered our way through secondary school and we all went to St Judes Church youth club in Balham, every Friday evening. That's where music started to come into my life.

We all went to "Youth Clubs" in those days. They were the only place we could go to meet with people of our own age. We could play snooker, table tennis, darts, and chat-up the girls! I wasn't much good at that. We had a record player that someone brought from home so we could have a dance if we wanted to. There was always a person from the church in the canteen and the choirmaster was around too. He was a great bloke! He took us into the church and played Johnny & The Hurricanes "Red River Rock" with us on the mighty church organ.

In those days, when one of us bought a new record (vinyl to you) we could all listen to it together and talk about a "great drum break" or "guitar solo" while the girls swooned over the likes of Elvis, Ricky Nelson, etc. Remember at this time Cliff Richard hadn't started really. Nowadays all our youngsters have their headphones in and listen alone. Something's missing there. They aren't able to discuss anything together.

My Dad had given me an old violin, which I had succeeded in producing sounds akin to crucifying a cat! Then my sister Barbara's friend Marian, gave me a Ukelele Banjo that belonged to an elderly member of her family. Now this instrument made sense to me and made a good sound. I taught myself a few chords and joined the school traditional jazz band.

Now this "band" consisted of Drums, Tea-chest Bass, Banjo, (that was me,) Piano Accordion and a Trumpet or Cornet, I'm not too sure. It was awful! Thankfully, Lonnie Donegan came on the scene and we all branched off to form Skiffle

Groups. This was 1957. Rock'n'Roll had just begun but Skiffle was easier to play.

I sold my Hornby Dublo train set to buy a guitar for eight pounds and ten shillings. Massive regrets in later years but if I hadn't, I would never have got into music. I knew about five chords so I sort of ran a guitar class at the youth club and our first group THE SKYLINERS came out of that.

Bern and Pete played guitar, Dave played the tea-chest bass, a bloke called Terry Bott, played washboard and I sort of played the tuney, fill-in bits on guitar. I suppose that was the beginning of me being a "Lead Guitarist". We thought we were great but we were probably awful too!

Several boys came and went from the group but the original four of us stayed as a sort of nucleus. Two of Pete's cousins, one called Dave, the other Michael were in the group at one time. One of them brought along a quite good-looking blond-haired bloke from The Bec School called Michael Scheuer. He couldn't sing for nuts, couldn't play his guitar and he had such a superiority complex that he had to go. The democratic way of getting someone out of a band in those days, was to say, "Me and the lads have been having a chat………………." Or "Step one pace forward all members of this Skiffle Group. Where are you going so-and-so?"

Several years later, he had a top-ten hit under the name of MIKE SARNE. That was "Come Outside". Sung in a pseudo cockney accent nothing like the public school accent, which was how he really spoke. Wendy Richards, from *Are You Being Served*, was on that record with him.

THE SKYLINERS used to play not only at our youth club but we got a contract to play at kids "Saturday Morning Cinemas". We travelled all over London and the South East of England. This we thought was the big time! The kids used to mob us for autographs. Brilliant!

As we were all too young to drive in those days, Pete's Dad, Bill Mills, (great name that), used to ferry us around and one day a friend of his came to pick us up in an old Fordson van. On our way to one of the cinema gigs, we had to drive through a crowded market. It was a bit tight between a wall and a parked lorry but Bill's mate said, "That'll be alright". So, we're all sitting in the back on the floor (strictly illegal these days) when there's a "graunching" sound on one side behind us and it's starting to get draughty.

The Skyliners Skiffle Group at Tooting (I'm second from the left)

The van had caught on of the lorry's drop-down hinges and was winding out a piece of metal and inch wide like undoing a sardine tin! We couldn't go back so we had to carry on squeezing through.

We all laughed ourselves silly.

Around this time, BUDDY HOLLY, came to the U.K.
Several mates and I from school went to see him at The

The Skylinders Skiffle Group Poster

Trocadero, Elephant & Castle and were completely
knocked out. Next day, back at school, everyone wanted to

make a Fender Sratocaster. Well, we'd never seen anything like it in this country.

Headquarter and General Supplies Guitar advertisement

We all had to play inferior instruments bought from Headquarters & General Supplies because we couldn't afford the Hofners that Tommy Steele and Bert Weedon were playing. Woodwork class was amazing. Boys were drawing Strat shapes and sawing them out like mad. All except one. Me! I told Mr "Woody" Wendon, our teacher that I wanted to make a double bass like Buddy's Joe Maudin played! He, although shocked, said "O.K". So I drew it in chalk on the floor and off I went. Without "Woody's" help I would never have made it but I did. And it worked! It only had two real strings because the tension was too much. The other two were just ordinary string.

The funny thing is, I never meant to play this bass. It was for Dave Elliot to play. He did it very well and as it was the right shape it did look like the real thing.

I'll tell you one hilarious story about that bass. We were playing at Dalston, in East London, at the Classic Cinema for the kids Saturday morning show. For some unknown reason, we were wearing masks, *Lone Ranger* style. We came out of the underground station and were on the Zebra crossing when, *CRASH!* Dave, who was carrying the bass in a harness on his back, had stepped off the kerb, caught the spike in his turn-up and fallen flat on his face in the middle of the crossing. He looked like a tortoise, unable to get up and he still had the spike in his turn-up.

Luckily there was no damage to the bass or Dave. When we'd finished creasing up, we got him up and went off to do the gig.

We played at The Elephant & Castle Trocadero Theatre in a

massive skiffle group competition along with about 20

Homemade Bass for The Skyliners

other groups. Apparently, CLIFF RICHARD (Harry Webb) and his first group, who were entered in the competition, offered to play as "guest artists" but were told, "No Thanks".

The VIPERS SKIFFLE GROUP with WALLY WHYTON, were the stars of the show and I remember what a nice bloke Wally was. Unfortunately, we didn't win the contest. I think it was probably due to the fact that my voice had not yet broken and Lonnie Donegan songs sounded like Minnie Mouse instead!

We played a song recorded by Don Lang, from the *6.5 Special* TV show, called "White Silver Sands". Bern & Pete were to sing it like The Everly Brothers. They were very nervous and when they went to stage front, centre, Bern almost fell into the orchestra pit from his side of the mike. He hadn't noticed the mike was standing on its own little bit of stage, out from the main part. Pete just saved him from a catastrophe.

One Sunday lunchtime, we were due to play at a pub in Honiton in South East London. The landlord asked us to do a "play on & off" for a comedian. No problem. When this bloke appeared, he was about six feet four inches tall with a bright red beard BUT he was in school uniform! Grey cap, grey jacket, short trousers, one sock up, one down, horizontal striped tie, even the snake-hook belt that we wore as kids. He sounded really weird with a high-pitched, strangled voice. We thought he was nuts.

Years later, I was watching Michael Parkinson's show with

Peter Sellers as a guest. He told the story of this massive bloke with a red beard who turned up on his doorstep in a Boy Scout uniform, on a bike, in the rain, soaked to the skin. He said to Peter, Spike Milligan says I'm a genius and I want to be a Goon. There he was! Our massive schoolboy. Same bloke. Name, RUXTON HAYWOOD. He apparently was the inspiration for the voice of "Bluebottle". On reflection I can totally understand why.

Ruxton Haywood

In the summer of 1958, the West London area known as Soho, had an event called strangely enough, The Soho Fair and we managed to get an entry into The Soho Fair Vocal Group Competition. We already had begun an affair with harmony singing so we decided to go with just me on guitar and the others just singing. So all dressed in matching shirts and ties we were going to be just like THE DALLAS BOYS from the top TV show *Oh Boy!* weren't we? Wrong!

We were set to sing "26 Miles," a FOUR PREPS song. All worked out and choreographed so that after two verses we'd turn to face the other way. Anyway after the <u>first</u> verse, I turned round on my own and there I was, face to face with Terry Bott. Pete had done the same and was standing nose to nose with Bern. How we didn't just burst out laughing I'll never know. Anyway we got through it after about 27 repeats of the last line because we couldn't remember how to finish it.

One of the judges was PETER NOBLE who used to present *Movie-Go-Round* on the BBC Radio Light Programme. He thought we were very good but I seem to remember he rather liked the fresh-faced young teenage boys a bit too

31

much.

That competition was won by the excellent EMILE FORD and THE CHECKMATES. They performed their "What Do You Want To Make Those Eyes At Me For" and completely blew away all the other contestants. Just great! Four weeks later, EMILE was top of the Hit Parade and justifiably so. A really nice bloke and a consummate professional.

During that time on Jan 22nd 1961, we also got to play at The 2 I's coffee bar, which of course was the place where so many rock'n'pop stars began their careers by being discovered. Guys like Tommy Steele. Hank Marvin & Bruce Welch met Cliff Richard there too.

I just remember it as being absolutely packed solid, hot and sweaty but a fantastic atmosphere for music. Who knows, the famous LARRY PARNES who had a "stable" of rock'n'roll singers, might have been there and couldn't get through the crowd to sign us up. When we weren't playing, we would still go there to soak up the music that came up from the cellar through the fan-light windows at pavement level. That was one hell of an exciting time to be a teenager.

We had a small music shop at the bottom of Balham Hill called Watkins Music. The proprietor was CHARLIE WATKINS. The man who invented "The Watkins Copicat" echo box. A marvellous piece of equipment that produced the Shadows (Drifters) guitar sounds that an ordinary kid could afford. Not Like the Vox or the Binson. They were way out of my league money-wise. I had the second or third one that Charlie made and it lasted me years until I lost it in Germany some years later. Worth quite a lot of money to a collector today. I also had a Watkins Westminster 10 watt amp and a triangular Watkins Dominator, which was the one that prompted Mo Foster to call his book *17 Watts*? because that was its power rating.

Pete Mills had the first Watkins Rapier guitar. Charlie came out of his workshop at the back and said, "What do you think of this boys?" It wasn't that good but again Pete could afford it. He always said it had a neck like a cricket bat with strings. It looked a bit like a Gibson SG then. With fluted edges, pointed cutaways and dark varnish finish with a pearlized scratch plate, but evolved into the Stratocaster shape that every guitar collector knows today. If Pete still had it, it would be worth quite a lot of money but there you go. Charlie went on, to head the successful company called WEM. Watkins Electric Music. Once again, his P.A. equipment was always affordable and good stuff. Nice man Charlie.

Sometime around there, we played as support act to JOHNNY DUNCAN and The BLUE GRASS BOYS. Johnny had a monster hit with "Last Train To San Fernando". His guitarist, Brian Daly was unwell so they asked me to play with them. Was I out of my depth or what? I'm sure I made a right pigs ear out of it and couldn't wait to get off. Luckily it was only a small venue like a village hall or something so I couldn't have upset too many people.

We did a gig at Wandsworth Town Hall, opposite The Technical college, where I would later study. We were supporting two DJs who worked on Radio Caroline and were fast becoming famous. One was DAVE CASH, the other KENNY EVERETT. Kenny was so funny and clever with all his jingles and lunatic stuff. You could see then how he would make it to the top later. They introduced an "up-and-coming" star of the future named JONATHAN KING. His record "Everyone's Gone To The Moon" later would top the charts. He didn't impress us nor did he talk to us so I'll leave it at that. I met Kenny again some years later but I'll come to that too.

We had a lot of fun in THE SKYLINERS but time moved on musically and Terry had to go, along with his washboard. CLIFF RICHARD and the SHADOWS were making changes to the music scene. We needed drums, so Bern bought some. Dave Elliot had gone into the law as a career and left the band, so I recruited a new friend from Wandsworth Technical College where I was studying to become a telecom engineer. That was Dennis Rafferty, a lovely Irish lad with a lunatic sense of humour. He played bass guitar so now we were off and running. We also had a new name, THE JOKERS.

Now THE JOKERS were quite a good band but the trouble was there were so many bands around with about the same ability. We did the usual round of local venues and had a good time doing it. Once we entered a competition at The Gaumont State Theatre in Kilburn.

We had to play one instrumental and one vocal. Pete sang Elvis' "Mess Of Blues" and I played lead on "Apache". What we didn't realise was, one of the judges was JERRY LORDAN who had written the damned thing for THE SHADOWS! We managed to come second and won a cheque for about £50. I felt quite embarrassed shaking hands with Mr. Lordan after we had probably crucified his tune. The other judge was LES REED (Johnny Worth) who was another successful songwriter of the time.

Dennis and I wanted to expand our horizons but Bern and Pete didn't feel they could. So unfortunately we split up. I'm very pleased we're all still very good friends.

The Jokers presentation at State Kilburn - receiving 2nd prize from Les Reed & Jerry Lordan

Dennis and I answered an ad in the *Melody Maker* and got a

job in a band called Bobby King and The Orbits over in Woolwich, which didn't last long basically because the singer couldn't sing! He was a 'pretty boy' and that was about it really. We formed another band from those who had auditioned, dragged Pete Mills in from the old band and called it THE CON MEN. A very appropriate name!

We did a gig at Kew, in The Boathouse alongside the river Thames. The main band was CLIFF BENNETT and THE REBEL ROUSERS. What a band that was! CLIFF on vocals, MICKEY BURT (later with Chas & Dave) on drums, FRANKIE ALLEN (later with The Searchers) on bass, MICK KING on guitar and SID PHILLIPS on Tenor sax and piano. Now that band knew how to play Rock'n'Roll! On the night we played there, there was a fight and two "bouncers" picked up a guy by the collar and the arse of his trousers, and threw him off the balcony into The Thames. How he missed the towpath I don't know but it was funny at the time. THE CON MEN didn't last long and Dennis and I went our separate ways.

Chapter 4   The Packabeats

April 15th 1962

I saw an ad in the *Melody Maker*, which said: Wanted, Lead Guitarist and Bass Player for working band. Willing to Rehearse, Record and Travel.

That was THE PACKABEATS and my first real introduction as to how a professional band can play.

They had had a small chart hit (No. 49) with the instrumental "Gypsy Beat" on the Parlophone label but the original guitarist and bassist wanted to quit so I auditioned along with Ted Harvey on bass and we both got the job. I knew they were serious because at the audition, I had to play "Take Good Care Of My Baby" in Eb! Now in those days nobody played in Eb!

THE PACKABEATS line-up was Ian "Stoo" Stewart (the founder member) on drums, Derrick Leach keyboards, Tony Holland vocals plus Ted Harvey & Me. We all hit it off straight away and the gigs began to pour in.

The Packabeats

Malcolm Lenny

Tony Holland

40

We were semi-pro at the time so it was not uncommon to do a days work at our normal jobs and then drive to somewhere like Rocky Rivers Rock'n'Roll Club in Bedford to do a gig, get home at two am and get up for work again at seven thirty am! We used to play with so many other bands who were doing the same sort of thing as us. We would frequently play at Southall Community Centre in West London along with Cliff Bennett & the Rebel Rousers, Brian Poole & The Tremeloes, Tony Rivers & The Castaways, Terry Franks & The Avalons, Jackie Lynton & The Teenbeats, Jimmy Justice's Jury to name just a few! It was RICKY WEST of The Tremeloes who showed me how to bend guitar strings like my idol James Burton from the early Ricky Nelson recordings. Simple really, just put on two E strings for E & B and move all the rest down, to using a fifth for a sixth etc.

Jackie Lynton had the brilliant ALBERT LEE playing lead guitar for him at one time. A lovely bloke, and a hell of a good guitarist. Albert has become one of the most respected players of all time and at the time of writing he still tours the U.K. with The Everly Brothers every time they come over. He's been on Eric Clapton's *Crossroads Show* from the USA. He's a regular member of Bill

Wyman's Rhythm Kings and he was part of *The Concert for George Harrison*, many years later.

One night at Southall, there was a band called Neil Christian & The Crusaders playing with us. They had a scrawny young kid of about 16 with a Gibson Les Paul hanging round his neck. They introduced him as "The Rock'n'Roll Champion of 1963". That was JIMMY PAGE and he could play a bit too!

TONY RIVERS went on to be one of Cliff Richard's backing singers and vocal arrangers in later years.

Terry Franks, of The Avalons, used to sing so hard and so high that he used to go scarlet in the face. He made us think he was going to explode if he didn't stop!

A regular band that we encountered was SCREAMING LORD SUTCH & THE SAVAGES. Now a lot of musicians played with Dave Sutch but at this particular time his guitarist, was a good-looking boy with a Gibson ES335TD Cherry. That was RITCHIE BLACKMORE. He looked quite funny in his Savage leopard skin spotted loin-cloth. But not as funny as me when I had to stand in for Ritchie when he was unwell one night! I was six foot two inches and weighed less than 10 stone. Not exactly a scary sight for the punters. I met Ritchie several more times during my musical career but I'll come to that later.

My very favourite story about Dave Sutch was that THE PACKABEATS were in London at the Sound City music shop, Shaftsbury Avenue, (Dave Dee & The Bostons were in there too) buying a new P.A. system when there was one hell of a commotion outside. We went out and there was Dave Sutch, driving a Land Rover, towing a piano on its castors!

"Where are you going Dave?" we shouted.

"Bedford", was his reply.

Now there's just no answer to that only to say that it was doubtable that he would have got past Piccadilly Circus without the piano falling apart.

We were sharing a gig with Sutch one night, when he was doing his "Jack The Ripper" routine. Dressed in top hat and cape, carrying his Gladstone bag, he chased Freddy "Fingers" Lee, his piano player, who was dressed as one of The Ripper's "Lady" victims, round the hall, back up onto the stage with a fearsome looking knife and once he had him backed up on top of the piano he was supposed to stab Freddy. He had a thick rubber pad under his "dress" but Sutch missed it and pierced Freddy nearly in the groin! There was claret everywhere! That was always the danger of working with Sutch, you stood a fair chance of getting killed. An almost complete loony, but Hey, the world needs more loonies. That's why he formed The Monster Raving Loony Party later on.

Southall Community Centre was an important venue to the "musos" of that period. We even got to play along with JET HARRIS & TONY MEEHAN after they had left the SHADOWS. I don't think BRIAN POOLE ever forgave TONY HOLLAND & THE PACKABEATS for finishing our set with "Do You Love Me", just before they came on. After all, they were in the top ten with it!

All the PACKABEATS plus wives and lovers went to Wallington Village Hall in Surrey to see the fantastic JERRY LEE LEWIS around this time. He was an absolute knockout! He was backed by THE OUTLAWS who were great too. I just wish we'd hung around to meet the great man afterwards but we didn't.

We were playing in West Ham one night and the support

band to us was STEVE MARRIOTT'S MOMENTS. Completely unknown outside their local area, but what a singer. It was obvious that Steve would go places! This was proven when he became part of The SMALL FACES later in his career. Steve really was a 'Geezer'.

Chapter 5   Making Records

The PACKABEATS hadn't made a record since "GYPSY
BEAT" for PARLOPHONE and we needed to get back into
the public eye and the "Hit Parade" as it was known then.
Our first effort was at the R.G.Jones Studio at Merton Park
Surrey. The original band had made demos there before
but I had never been in a real studio. It was great! We
recorded 10 songs, all with Tony Holland on lead vocals.
The sound wasn't that brilliant but Jones's had the most
amazing plate reverb unit. It was a disc about four feet in
diameter that the sound was passed through to give a
wide-open effect like the Albert Hall. It was housed in a
wooden cabinet on the wall in the corridor and controlled
by turning like a ship's wheel to increase or decrease the
amount of reverb. The ship's wheel was not small. It was as
big as a helmsman's wheel. We really liked those
recordings but, unfortunately, none of the record
companies did. I was working as an engineer for The GPO
in the Power Section at the time, which meant maintaining

all the ancillary equipment in the London Telephone Exchanges. I'd done a two year apprenticeship before qualifying. I think I have to tell the almost terrifying story of the time I was almost electrocuted. I was working on a big rectifier in an exchange somewhere in London. The rectifier was the piece of equipment, which charged the emergency batteries that every exchange had as a standby in case of a power failure. I had turned off the power and put one of our red enamel plated signs on the mains supply. It said "WARNING. ENGINEERS WORKING. DO NOT TOUCH". So there I was, standing on a three foot pair of steps, leaning into the five foot square metal cased rectifier with a single ended, rubber-sleeved spanner. The nut was very stiff and it took all of my strength to loosen it. It gave way and my spanner shot round and hit the casing. What I didn't know was that some idiot had turned the mains back on! I got the full force of about 400 volts DC through me because the rubber sleeve had been cut through. Direct Current holds you on. Not like AC, which throws you off.

Luckily my work colleague saw me slumped over the casing with my limp legs dangling down. He hit the circuit breaker and cut off the power. Apparently I was unconscious for about 20 minutes. The local Doctor who was brought in to examine me said, "Young man after what's happened to you you'll probably live forever!" I was always doubly careful after that incident.

Generally working for The GPO was not too bad as jobs go but then, right out of the blue we had the offer to go professional as a band. My dear old Mum was terrified! The thing was, in those days, every town had a Mecca Ballroom or a Top Rank Dance Hall. Every Burton Tailors had a Dance Hall above it too, so a band could play every night of the week in a different town. Add that to the village halls, community centres and theatres and you were a working musician.

We had a Manager called Bob Alexander who once was an all-in wrestler of some repute. I believe he once part-owned a club opposite The 2 I's in Wardour Street called The Footprint Club. Bob's wife Jean, ran an agency. One day Bob said we had a recording booked with some up-and-coming record producer up in London. That turned out to be the amazing Mr. Joe Meek!

Now Joe had his "studio" above a leather bag shop in 304, Holloway Road, North London. He was just about having his world-wide, monster hit, "TELSTAR" by THE TORNADOS. Loads of stories have been told about the legendary Joe Meek so I'll just tell you mine.

Joe Meek

The session was booked to record two instrumentals. Tony was not involved in these. His turn was to come later. Joe had sent us a tune played by either him or Geoff Goddard on piano with probably some of his "house band" The OUTLAWS. The tune to be the A side was all played on the black notes but quite a nice melody. We had made an arrangement which we thought was OK and thankfully Joe liked it too. He was notorious for losing his temper with all sorts of people over almost nothing at all. He even made me sing a high falsetto bit at the end that sounded like a choirboy. We were totally unaware of Joe's sexual preferences at that time. So it didn't matter. The only odd thing was that Joe always wore a suit and tie whenever we saw him. Nothing wrong with that.

Derrick played the tune on his Hohner Cembalet. It didn't have a title but we thought it sounded vaguely French so, with typical musicians humour, we called it "French Porridge". Not exactly a catchy title I hear you cry. With a bit more thought, Stoo's wife Eileen came up with "EVENING IN PARIS". Brilliant!

The B side was the theme from a pretty awful British B film called *THE TRAITORS*. The film starred Patrick Allen. Better known then as the Barrett Homes commercial bloke. It was a good tune but weak. By the time we, and Joe, had finished with it, it was Fantastic! It drove along and sounded like it was good enough to be a hit record. Joe scared me a bit when I'd just finished playing it and he came out of the other room rubbing his hands together with glee and said, "That was great. Now play it again on the other pick-up and GET IT RIGHT!" No pressure there then.

Luckily I did get it right and he used it as double-tracking to fatten up the sound.

How the hell Joe got such great sounds out of his gear set up in the second bedroom of his flat with the living room being used as the studio. There were various carpets all over the floor to act as sound depressants. I remember well Stoo was in the bay window with his drums. Behind him was a mattress or two to deaden the sound. A Chinese screen separated him from the rest of the room. I sat in front of the window opposite the door with my Vox AC30 amp mic'd up beside me. Derrick sat with his back to Joe's legendary out-of-tune piano. Ted, on Bass, sat on the landing outside Joe's control room (second bedroom).

Stoo never quite got over Joe's play-back speaker cabinet, which stood in front of the fireplace. It was a monster! Like a double wardrobe with one or more speakers in it that made playback so exciting that your ears bled, you wet yourself and your hair stood on end. No wonder dear old

Mrs Violet Shenton, who owned the shop downstairs, used to complain about the noise.

So we had two really good tracks ready for release. Joe took them to PYE records who said yes but they, and Joe, wanted "EVENING IN PARIS" to be the A side. After all he had written it! We didn't care, we were getting a record out at last.

It was adopted by the perfume company who made Evening in Paris, for their show on Radio Luxembourg, which I think went out three or four times a week.

We heard it played on various request shows like *Housewives Choice* etc. I can't explain how exciting it is to be sitting at home or in the group van and your record comes on the radio. You really feel that you've made it. Paris was doing really well by way of sales and had reached number 38 in the *RECORD MIRROR* chart.

In those days, there was the *New Musical Express, Melody Maker, Disc & Music Echo* and *Record Mirror.* All with their own Hit Parade.

We had sold about 13,000 records when, what happened? PYE Records went on strike! For three weeks they didn't

Evening In Paris/The Traitors Pye 45 rpm

press any more 45s and by the time they went back to work we were dead in the water.

Oh well, that's the way the cookie crumbles.

THE PEOPLE

NEWCOMERS

Brightest of the new beat groups to assault my ears are **The Packabeats**, whose debut disc on the Pye label is one of the best instrumentals I have heard for some time.

"Evening In Paris" has a distinct French flavour, while "The Traitors" comes from the film of the same name. **Malcolm Lenny's** solo guitar is heard to advantage, and to me this sounds like a cert for Top Twenty honours.

Packabeats may be on a big hit

The Packabeats

Evening In Paris; The Traitors
(Pye N 15480)★★★★

THE drummer—and leader—Ian Stewart is the only member left of the original Packabeats quartet which was formed about four years ago. He should be glad he persevered because, with Joe Meek's help he could well be on a big hit.

The instrumental outfit has a couple of guitars, drums and a brilliant front noise supplied by something which sounds like an organ yet isn't, if you know what I mean!

It's called a Cambelet. Using this, and the RGM Studios sound, on a Meek composition "Evening In Paris," the group have an ear-clutching release that deserves big sales.

"The Traitors" is a Johnny Douglas composition for the film of the same title. Great dark guitar sound on this half.

DISC

Press clippings for "Evening In Paris"/"The Traitors" release

PACKABEATS

Evening In Paris; The Traitors (Pye 15480)

FROM the boys who gave us "Gypsy Beat" comes this merry little Joe Meek composition. Played with the usual instruments, the lead is taken by guitar, and a chorus joins in about half-way through. Not bad, but not chart material.

Flip is the theme from the film. It moves at a faster tempo than the top side, but lacks the commercial appeal. Well-performed on a lower key than the first side.

THREE 🔔🔔🔔

RECORD MIRROR

We returned back to Joe's some months later to record another two instrumentals. This time we'd re-worked Bobby Darin's "DREAM LOVER" but Joe did one of his things to it where he recorded both of Derrick's keyboards and sped one up (for effect). The result was a half tone out of tune and jeez!, it put my teeth on edge every time I heard it. Painful but it did have a great guitar solo on it even though I say it myself! When Joe saw my new Gibson ES335TD Cherry, he decided to use the same(ish) sound that he'd just used for RITCHIE BLACKMORE earlier on that day on a vocal he's just recorded with HEINZ BURT from THE TORNADOS.

I actually passed RITCHIE on the stairs on the way up to do that recording. That was the second time I'd rubbed shoulders with him and not the last either!

The B side was another of Joe's compositions, which he called "PACKABEAT". Not a very original title but it was only a B side. Stoo did some great drumming on that track.

That record hardly saw the light of day but it wasn't very good anyway.

Tony Holland got his chance when dance crazes took off.

Ted and Stoo wrote a thing called "SIDEWALK" which was like the Hully Gully and the kids liked it. In we went to Joe's once more and recorded it. EMI liked it and gave Tony a one record contract. Bob Alexander added his name to the songwriters contract, much to Ted and Stoo's disgust. But then Bob was always out for a quick buck if he could make it.

The record got good publicity from the likes of Frank & Peggy Spencer's Dancing Schools and it was always on Radio Luxembourg (208 Metres on the medium wave) but it didn't take off unfortunately. The B side was a really nice song Joe gave us that was to have been Mike Berry's follow-up to his hit "Don't You Think It's Time" called "TIME GOES BY". That would have been a good first record for Tony. A really strangled version with Joe "singing" appeared many years later in a BBC TV *Arena* documentary. Tony also got an appearance on the top pop TV show of the day *THANK YOUR LUCKY STARS*. He had to mime to the record and we THE PACKABEATS were not allowed to appear with him because we were with a different record company and we weren't named on the actual label. We attended the show but had to sit in the audience. It was a good show featuring BRENDA LEE,

RONNIE CARROLL, MIKE SARNE (what him again!),
JULIE GRANT, SOUNDS INCORPORATED, Disc Jockey
JIMMY YOUNG and a new unknown group called GERRY
and the PACEMAKERS.

> **THANK YOUR LUCKY STARS:**
> With Brenda Lee, Ronnie Carroll, Mike Sarne, Julie Grant, Sounds Incorporated, Gerry and the Pacemakers, Tony Holland, and disc jockey Jimmy Young.

Tony Holland billed on Thank Your Lucky Stars

Three weeks after the show, GERRY was top of the charts
with "How Do You Do It?" We got to meet everyone even
though we weren't actually on the show. The good thing
from ours, and the promoter's point of view was that we
could be billed as TONY HOLLAND (HMV Recording
Artist) AND THE PACKABEATS (PYE Recording Artists)

We were booked to do a BBC Radio Light Programme (as it
was in those days) show called *The Talent Spot*. Just as the
title suggests, it was for new virtually unknown artistes
who had a record out and needed a plug. It was introduced
by a singer/presenter named Gary Marshall and along with
us, promoting his first record, "Air Travel" was the mighty

CHRIS FARLOWE, later to have a massive hit with "Out of Time". The resident band was The Ted Taylor 4. Their backing for Chris was "interesting". Using a Clavioline to play the Sax part sounded weird and I'll leave it at that other than to add that their version of "Desafinado" (slightly out of tune) was slightly out of tempo! The bass player hadn't quite got the feeling of the Bossa Nova beat. Even us new young professionals couldn't help but wince a bit. We got to play both sides of our single "Evening In Paris" & "The Traitors". Tony sang "Sidewalk" & Joe Brown's "It Only Took A Minute."

I met CHRIS FARLOWE again many years later when he was guesting on The Manfreds Show at The Tunbridge Wells Assembly Hall. In the interval, all the artists were in the foyer flogging their latest and greatest albums. I sidled up to Chris and said, "I was on the BBC show called *The Talent Spot* with you when we were both just out of short trousers Chris." He looked at me and asked, who I was with. I told him THE PACKABEATS. He said (and I quote), "F**K Me! I remember that gig! How are you man? Are you still playing?" I gave him an edited version of what I'd been doing, after a massive bear hug, a crunching handshake off he went to do the second half of the show. Chris is still the

Sarf London Boy that he always was and good for him.

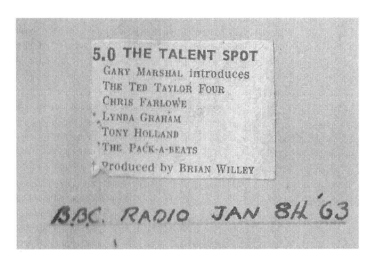

BBC Talent Spot Radio Times

Chapter 6   Gigging With The Packabeats

Work was piling in for THE PACKABEATS in our canary yellow stage jackets made by the great Cecil Gee of Shaftsbury Avenue and we were travelling all over the country. We did promotional things for the records like BBC TV *Juke Box Jury* where the great DAVID JACOBS wore a dinner jacket and black tie to present the show. No one could see that he had sand coloured jeans and open toed sandals under the desk. We were behind the screen on one show and we were voted "a miss" by the jury, who consisted of David Nixon, Barbara Kelly, Pete Murray and Josephine Douglas. Not exactly "happening people" but that's the way it was back then. I had another "shoulder rubbing" with Pete Murray later on too.

We also did an interview for Radio Luxembourg, which was gate-crashed by a couple of very drunk Pop Stars - BRIAN JONES of The Rolling Stones and ERIC BURDON of The Animals. They didn't do themselves any favours and were not our favourite people after that.

We played at ROCKY RIVERS TOP TEN CLUB in Bedford where we met the great BARRON KNIGHTS. They were such a good band long before they had their hit records. On one particular night, their 36 seater bus broke down and the five of them and us five PACKABEATS were all pushing it like mad down the street at 1am in the morning laughing our heads off, trying to be quiet.

Sometime later, Tony Avern, manager of the BARRON KNIGHTS, offered me a chance to join them but I declined, thinking that THE PACKABEATS were on their way to the stars. However, I'm pretty certain I could never have been as funny or musically clever as BUTCH BAKER who did join them.

Another night at The Top Ten Club had JOE BROWN supporting us (on less money) and he was in the charts with "A Picture Of You" but he'd been booked a long time before he became famous. So he honoured his contract. Great bloke Joe.

We did a night at Dunstable California Pool where GEORGIE FAME and the BLUE FLAMES were top of the bill, BILLY J. KRAMER and the DAKOTAS were second and we, TONY HOLLAND and the PACKABEATS were last.

We were helping Georgie and his guys up the long front steps with his Hammond Organ when someone tripped and dropped his end! It crashed down onto the concrete steps and Georgie's Conga player, Speedy Aquai, turned his hands upwards and said, "Obla De Obla Da." I swear that's where that phrase came from for The BEATLES song later on. It really does mean, Life Goes On, So What.

On stage that night, Billy J. wanted us to move all of our gear off the stage before he came on. He was in the charts at the time with "Do You Want To Know A Secret" so he thought he warranted special treatment. We said, "No way". Because we had another spot to do after Georgie Fame who was on the other stage. Anyway, once Billy J. saw how well we'd gone down with the punters, he conceded and we all became friends again. I didn't know, until he told me, that The Dakotas drummer, Tony Mansfield was Elkie Brooks' brother!

We played one night down at the Clarence Pier Ballroom in Southsea along with BILLY FURY. The support band was

DAVE DEE & THE BOSTONS later to become DAVE DEE, DOZY, BEAKY, MICK, TITCH, SLEEPY, GRUMPY, DOC & BASHFUL. Billy was very nervous and we did laugh when we saw him roll up a handkerchief, longways, and put it down the front of his trousers. Now why would he have done that? I can't imagine. He went down well anyway. He would, because he was a good performer.

We played at what can only be called a massive out-door pop festival in Hayes, Middlesex. We had to back MICKEY MOST as well as do our own act. I won't go through the whole cast list but here's a running order of the programme so you can see. It wouldn't be financially possible to put together a show like this these days. The cost would be astronomical!

LONDON'S GREATEST EVER
OPEN AIR POP FESTIVAL

WHIT MONDAY, 3rd JUNE 1963

Your Guest Comperes for the afternoon:
PAT CAMPBELL, Star Disc Jockey from the B.B.C.
and Radio Luxembourg.

GARY MARSHALL, singing compere from the B.B.C.'s "Talent Spot" assisted by Botwell's favourite Disc Jockey — TONY YOUNG

11.00am	Show opens with the BLUE DIAMONDS
11.30am	REY ANTO & M SQUAD
12.00am	MICK MOST
12.15pm	THE GOLLI-GOLLI BOYS
12.20pm	JIMMY CRAWFORD & THE RAVENS
12.25pm	JOHNNY, MIKE & THE SHADES
12.55pm	JACKIE LYNTON & THE TEENBEATS
1.15 pm	THE CRESTERS
1.35pm	ROBB STORME & THE WHISPERS
1.40pm	DEL SHANNON
1.50pm	CHERRY ROLAND
2.00pm	CLIFF BENNETT & THE REBEL ROUSERS
2.30 pm	KENNY LYNCH
2.50 pm	GERRY & THE PACEMAKERS
3.20 pm	SCREAMING LORD SUTCH & HIS SAVAGES
3.50 pm	BILLY J. CRAMER & THE DAKOTAS
3.55 pm	EDEN KANE
4.05 pm	TONY HOLLAND & THE PACKABEATS
4.35 pm	VINCE TAYLOR & THE PLAYBOYS

5.05 pm   FREDDIE & THE DREAMERS

5.35 pm   BRIAN POOLE & THE TREMELOES

Programme subject to alteration

The outdoor stage was a wobbly thing made from scaffolding and planking. We were all warned to be careful. Screaming Lord Sutch be careful? No way! Dave Sutch had attached a long rope to the scaffold pole in the middle of the stage. He ran on stage, grabbed the rope and swung out over the first 10 rows of people and the stage swung round too! We thought that was it, but thankfully it held out throughout the whole day.

TED HARVEY decided to leave the band about now and we auditioned a lovely guy from Sheffield by the name of GARY UNWIN. He had been playing with the resident Mike Rabin Band (Son of the great Dance Band Leader OSCAR RABIN) at the Wimbledon Palais and wanted a bit of fame and fortune. Having Gary in the band with his Yorkshire accent was weird mainly because we were a South London band. However, he was a bit of a magnet for the girls. A cute guy with blondish hair and a basin cut. Liverpool bands were the thing of the moment and Gary had a funny accent too!

The Packabeats group hug

On our way up to do a tour in Scotland, we had a gig in Birmingham. We were the famous recording stars so we had a local band supporting us. They were CARL WAYNE and The BEACHCOMBERS. Later, to become THE MOVE then WIZZARD, then ELO etc. They were excellent. Carl on vocals, ROY WOOD, BEV BEVAN and I think JEFF

67

LYNNE was there but I'm not sure.We were sharing a revolving stage. They had one half and we had the other.

The Packabeats on stage at Hitchin with Gary Unwin

We asked which way the stage revolved and they told us. So we laid out all our cables for the P.A. and our amps all neatly and ready for the off. Well, when the tit was pushed, off went the stage in the opposite direction unplugging all our gear so we came round to the audience with Stoo thrashing away on his drums and nothing else. Those bloody BEACHCOMBERS were laughing their heads off! It was a great joke and that's how we took it. They were good blokes and we would probably have done the same to them if we'd had a chance.

The first night on that Scottish tour was in Perth, in a very large and scary old theatre. It was a total sell-out and the bill was topped by THE SEARCHERS. All the original members were there. TONY JACKSON, MIKE PENDER, JOHN McNALLY & CHRIS CURTIS. They were having monster hit records at the time and went down a storm.

We did very well with our spot but we were very impressed by a band at the bottom of the bill called THE FORTUNES with The Cliftones. Yes, it was the original FORTUNES of "Caroline" - "You've Got Your Troubles" - "Here It Comes Again" etc. They were vocally excellent long before they had hits. I bumped into several of the guys on that show much later in my career.

The tour was based in the small town of Elgin, in Morayshire. We worked for a man by the name of ALBERT BONICI, an ex-pat Italian Scot! A complete nut but fun to work for. He had his office in an ice cream parlour with a

—THE SEARCHERS - - -

PAISLEY, 1963

Souvenir
1/-

Presented by Albert A. Bonici and Andy Lothian, Junior

The Searchers Paisley programme photo 1963

dance hall above called, The Two Red Shoes. Albert had the claim to fame that he had already got THE BEATLES booked to play at The Two Red Shoes before they hit the charts with "Love Me Do". The story goes that he paid them the princely sum of £65 and they were in the top 20!

We played there of course but it was a nine day tour so we got around a bit. In Inverness, we met ANITA HARRIS, whose career was just taking off. She had her Mum in tow just in case any of us virile young popsters had any ideas! After all, she was a very pretty young girl and friendly, when you could get near her. That show was a midnight matinee and, true to it's title, didn't start until midnight. A Scottish band were supporting the named artists. They were called THE CRESTERS. A good band with a strong lead vocalist who amazed me by putting a teaspoon full of Vicks Vapour Rub in his mouth to combat sore throats! I think, that must have been the beginning of hard drugs in Scotland. You had to be hard to do that!

One of the smaller towns we played in was Craigallachie. Now that's a name that doesn't slip easily off the tongue. Listening to Tony asking a local resident where it was in his Sarf London accent was hilarious. Craigallachie turned out to have a special meaning to THE PACKABEATS, because, after we finished our first set, we were having a cup of tea in the kitchen when someone came in and said, "President Kennedy has been killed in Dallas". What? We didn't believe it. But it was true. Everyone was in total shock. That sort of thing just didn't happen. But it had happened. The dance was cancelled and everyone left the hall in silence. They say that everyone knows where they were when Kennedy died. Well, THE PACKABEATS were in that little town in Scotland.

We did two nine or ten day trips to Scotland and had a great time but I do have to say that The Beach Ballroom at Aberdeen, must rate amongst the coldest places in the world. I think that was the night I went on stage in my sheepskin jacket!

On the way back, we played in Lowestoft (the second coldest place in Great Britain) alongside a Nothern band called THE CHEROKEES. They were such a funny bunch. There were, I think seven of them and the stage wasn't that big to take all the gear of both bands. Mainly because there was a concert-size grand piano at one end. So, we got permission to take it off. Easier said than done! Now, grand pianos are VERY heavy. The stage was about four feet high so it had to be lifted off at chest height and kept level. I think we were all helping to lift and the moment we got the tail-end off the stage, the leg fell off! No one wanted to let go to retrieve the lost leg. We were all too scared of letting it fall. What made it worse was, they all spoke like the Lancashire comedian, AL REID.

All you heard was - "From you, to me, Mind that leg, Coom on, all together, now lift!" It was hilarious. How we ever got it down without breaking it was nothing short of a miracle.

Eventually, THE PACKABEATS were not getting as many bookings as we had been getting. The Liverpool bands had grabbed the market place and coming from London didn't mean much any more. Plus they played for less money than we were used to. Derrick was the first to leave in July 1964. We tried to carry on as a four piece but it wasn't really working and a month or two later we decided to call it a day.

I had a great time with TONY HOLLAND and THE PACKABEATS. It was an excellent period in the music scene when anyone could go out almost any night of the week, to a local dance hall, village hall or theatre and see at least two bands. I got THE PACKABEATS together again many years later as will be revealed.

Chapter 7 The Hi-Fi's Recording And Touring

In August '64, I got a call from Ted Harvey, the ex-bass player from THE PACKABEATS, asking if I'd like to join his current band The HI-FI'S. Naturally I jumped at the chance. I didn't have a band to play with and I was crawling up the wall with frustration. I auditioned for them in a Scout hall called The Quest, in Newbury, South London. Great sound! And I got the job. The band was lead by Brian Bennett on keyboards, same name, different bloke. Malcolm Wright, known as Mel (?) on drums, Ted Harvey on bass and me on guitar. My first gig with The Hi-Fi's was in a big seafront house at Littlestone on the South Kent coast. I loved it. It was so musical. Brian was a great musician/singer and it all just gelled together. The second gig was at Royal Tunbridge Wells Assembly Hall as part of a package show featuring BIG DEE IRWIN who had a massive hit with "Swingin' On A Star" with LITTLE EVA. THE TORNADOS were also on that show. I think HEINZ BURT had left to go solo by then.

The HI-Fi's Battersea Park publicity shot
– very early morning and cold

Very quickly, we were rushed into a studio to record something, as we needed a record out. Brian and Ted had written their previous offerings "Take Me Or Leave Me" and "Will Yer Or Won't Yer" with small successes. This time, I suggested we record an old CHUCK JACKSON song written by Jerry Leiber & Mike Stoller called "I Keep Forgettin'" . Ted sang lead vocal and then wrote the B side in about 10mins. It was called "Kiss & Run". "A surfing kind of thing with a strong resemblance to "Da Do Ron Ron" by The Crystals". That's what the review in the *NME* said.

The session was engineered by an up-and-coming guy by the name of GLYN JOHNS. He made a great job of the recording and we had a great time. GLYN went on to record some of THE BEATLES later songs. He really knew what he was doing. He didn't rant and rave like dear old Joe Meek. He just pointed to a plaque on the wall that was attributed to MIKE D'ABO & The Band of Angels that said, "Take 17 and for God's sake RELAX!" Mike fronted MANFRED MANN later on.

"I Keep Forgettin'" got lots of radio plays and sold a few thousand but didn't make the charts, anyway, we liked it.

Then it was the time when a lot of us jobbing bands were given a LENNON & McCARTNEY song to record. MARMALADE got "Obla Di, Obla Da", THE OVERLANDERS got "Michelle". The Hi-Fi's got "Baby's In Black". Now don't get me wrong, it's a great song, but it's in 6/8 tempo (fast waltz) and the kids have to be able to dance to it. So, the others got hits, we didn't.

Hi-Fi'"Baby's In Black" advertising handbill

Hi-Fi's "I Keep Forgettin'" - NME front page

Here's a strange story about that recording. We were given the sheet music, not the record. When it came to the guitar solo, I played the first 4 bars almost identical to GEORGE HARRISON without hearing his solo! Creepy or what? Unfortunately, I didn't ever get to tell George that but I would've liked the chance.

I never got to meet The Beatles but I did meet the guy who cut some of their master discs at Abbey Road. Name, Malcolm Davis. Another lovely guy and a complete nutcase! He told me a great story about an American friend of his on a visit to Abbey Road. They went up to the front door and it was opened by none other than Paul

McCartney! Macca greeted Malc, asked what he was doing there. Malc told him that his friend was having a tour round the studios and Macca said, "I'll take him round if you like!" His mouth fell wide open with disbelief. That guy must've dined out on that story for years.

October '64 we had just been signed up to do a 6 nights a week, 3 week tour headed by

THE HOLLIES.

With HEINZ, the ex-Tornado,

JESS CONRAD, the incomparable,

THE DIXIE CUPS from U.S.A.

THE TORNADOS

WAYNE GIBSON & THE DYNAMIC SOUNDS

THE HI-FI'S

THE WILD BOYS

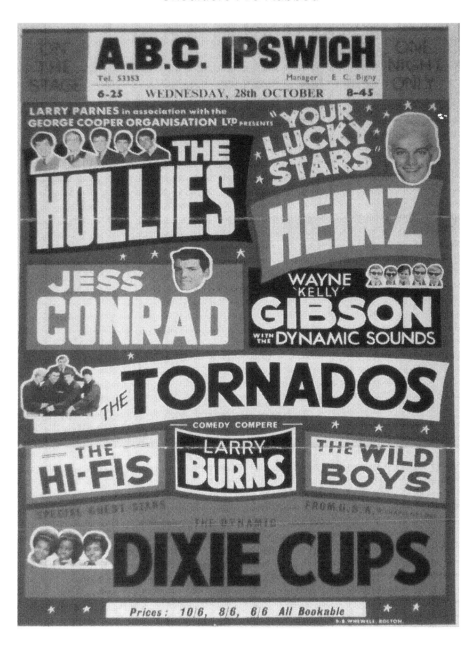

The Hi-Fi's Tour Poster 1964

This was a great show. It was all five original HOLLIES. ALLAN CLARKE, GRAHAM NASH, TONY HICKS, ERIC HAYDOCK & BOBBY ELIOTT.

The Wild boys backed HEINZ. The TORNADOS backed THE DIXIE CUPS and we backed JESS CONRAD.

Now don't laugh! Jess would be the first to say that he's wasn't a great singer but he was such a good-looking bloke with a really cheeky sense of humour that he went down a storm. It became a battle between Jess and Heinz as to who got the most screams from the girls in the audience.

Jess Conrad

At one of the shows, Jess stepped out on top of the mighty Wurlitzer Organ in the pit, to get closer to the girls. Not to be outdone, Heinz jumped onto it and went straight through the rigid plastic cover and there he stood up to his calves, unable to move. Brilliant!

Some of the highs from that tour were that THE HOLLIES were at number 5 with "We're Through" and we were on the front page of the *NME* advertising with "Keep Forgettin'" There was no danger of us knocking them off the top.

I was out getting a coffee with ALLAN CLARKE & HEINZ, when we, sorry they, were spotted by some girls. We ran! It didn't matter that I was a nobody. I was with two recognisable big names so I had to run too. We only just got back to the theatre or I'm pretty sure we'd have been torn to pieces. I might have enjoyed it. Who knows?

When we played Douglas Palace Theatre on The Isle of Man, we opened the second half of the show with The Four Seasons number "Rag Doll", I had the high falsetto voice. The opening bars were greeted with such screams from the crowd that the back of my neck still tingles when I think of it today. THE DIXIE CUPS weren't on the show that night because they had to do a TV show so we were joined by the great MARTY WILDE. I say great because he was such a consummate professional and handled his audience beautifully.

I think CLARKEY, as we all called him, had a birthday on that night, so JESS put on his best dinner suit, looking like a waiter and walked onto the stage with a bottle of champagne and glasses for six right in the middle of their act. Perfect timing? After the show, we all went to the casino. Some for a bet, most for a drink or three.

Now, the keyboard player of THE DYNAMIC SOUNDS was a blind guy named PETER COOK, who became known later as PETER LONDON and made records under that name. He became mates with ERIC HAYDOCK from THE HOLLIES. Those two and Mel Wright, known to us as Wrighty, and me, were in adjoining rooms in the hotel. After a few sherberts, it was time for bed. We all made our wobbly way up to our rooms. We shared a bathroom with those two and it was between the two rooms. We said our goodnights and watched them open the door to the bathroom and fall in the empty bath, rissed as pats so no one was hurt. Wrighty and I couldn't move them so there they stayed 'til the morning. Allegedly they had no memory of the event. Surprising really.

At one theatre, the HOLLIES tour manager was asking the stage manager for certain lighting plans for certain songs. He said, "You'd better talk to the lighting guy". He walked to stage front and called out, JEREMY!!! A voice in the darkness answered, "Yeeeees?". And this thing of beauty came to the stage front. All baggy jumper and open-toed sandals. Know what I mean? The tour manager started on about the lighting plans, coloured this and coloured that, when Jeremy interrupted him and said, "How d'you want them? On or off?" The lights were just white and on or off and that was that.

When the show reached Huddersfield, we had an amazing jam session on the stage after sound-check time. I forgot to mention that RITCHIE BLACKMORE was in The WILD BOYS backing HEINZ. We became quite good buddies for a while. The jam was RITCHIE, TONY HICKS, JIMMY O'BRIEN (Tornados Organist) CLEM CATTINI AND WRIGHTY on drums, TED HARVEY on bass and ME. Two drummers and three lead guitarists? Jeez did it rock!

It was a real shame when that tour ended because we had

all got on so well. No posers, no showing off, just musicians having a good time. Sitting on the tour bus with stars like The Hollies, all singing various songs together was what it was all about.

I forgot to mention that on the first day of the tour, we all met up at a London Transport canteen near Baker Street, before boarding the tour bus for the first date. There was another tour leaving on the same morning, which had been put together by the same promoter. That one starred LULU and The LUVVERS and MILLIE of "My Boy Lollipop" fame. LULU stood in front me in the breakfast queue ordering her nosh. Now, I'm a massive LULU fan but on that particular morning, she had her Glasgow face on. She must've been tired or something because, when the canteen lady put a couple of rubbery-looking eggs on her plate, she looked and said, "What the f**k's that?" In her raw Glaswegian accent. I creased up and so did she. Mind you, the food did look a bit suspect. It was more like a child's toy set of food from a cookery game.

LULU has developed into a truly great singer so I'm certain she can be forgiven for a small slip of the tongue on that miserable morning all those years ago.

The next Big thing we did was The Ideal Home Exhibition. The BBC used to have a stage there and transmit live shows every day on the old Light Programme as it was called before becoming Radio 1. We were on it with The BOB MILLER Band with DENNY PIERCEY - he used to compère *Easy Beat* on BBC Sunday morning radio. HEINZ again, DODI WEST, DYLLIS WATLING, PETE MURRAY.

Hi-Fi's at The Ideal Home Exhibition

If we'd known how big that show's audience was, I think we'd have been a bit scared.

December 5th '64 we did the top BBC radio show *SATURDAY CLUB* doing four songs and backing JESS CONRAD for another three again. The line-up was MARVIN GAYE, THE SEARCHERS, THE FOURMOST, THE SPOTNICKS. Unfortunately we didn't get to meet the others as the show was recorded on different days. I would've loved to have met the iconic MARVIN GAYE.

Brian Matthew -presenter of Saturday Club

BRIAN MATHEW was a really nice bloke who really knew his music. At the time of writing, he's still going strong with his *Sounds Of The Sixties* show on BBC Radio 2 on Saturday mornings. He's played my records quite a few times throughout the years and I've got a SOTS tee shirt! I had met THE FOURMOST many months before in a motorway café when I was with THE PACKABEATS. I know it sounds boring but they were all nice blokes.

Dec 11th '64 found us on *THE KATHY KIRBY SHOW*. She was such a lovely person and she was a massive star at the time. Her Manager, ex band leader Bert Ambrose, was a bit of a Svengali character, who was always in close attendance in case anybody made a move on Kathy. The show was recorded as live, that is, you heard what we played. That show was the night Kathy sang the song for the Eurovision Song Contest, "I Belong". The Director of the show was Ernest Maxin. He was a highly respected man who ran a very tight but fair ship.

That show had 13,000,000 viewers! I'm glad nobody told us that at the time. We played "Baby's In Black" and Kathy sang Ray Charles' song "What'd I Say?" with us backing her. It all sounded a bit thin until The Eric Robinson

Orchestra came in for the last 2 choruses. Wow! It blew us away. I couldn't believe the orchestra line-up. Ronnie Verrall, drums, Johnny Hawksworth, bass. Ivor Mirants, guitar, Kenny Baker, trumpet, Don Rendell, Ronnie Scott, saxes, Don Lusher, trombone.

Those are just the faces I recognised. It was about a 26-piece band so I'm sorry if I left anyone out.

I learned an important lesson about show business while on that showon that show. The wonderfully funny Harmonica act THE THREE MONARCHS were guest stars and during rehearsal, I stood in the wings watching them. There was a small table beside me with other harmonicas and props on it. I picked up a harmonica just to look at it when CEDRIC, the comedian of the group, said to me, "Don't ever touch anyone's props. You may spoil whatever they have set up for their next gag or song". He didn't say it in a nasty way but I absolutely took on board what he said and I apologised for touching anything. After all, I was a mere kid in a very big industry. That show was recorded as live and transmitted the following Saturday. We were booked to play at the Joe Lyons Corner House on the corner of Trafalgar Square on the night of transmission.

Kathy Kirby

Hi-Fi's outside the dressing room for Kathy Kirby TV Show

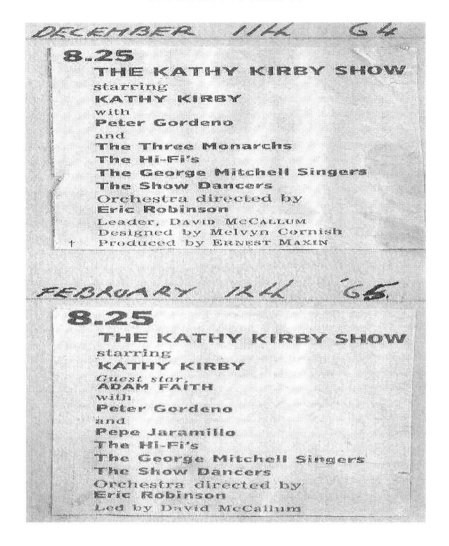

Hi-Fi's billing for Kathy Kirby TV Show

We got to see the show in a room above Lyons. It was totally brilliant to see ourselves and see how well we went down with the audience at the BBCTheatre, Shepherds Bush.

My Mum & Dad were in the audience that night. Right in the front row of the circle. One of Dad's work colleagues saw him and asked what he was doing there. Dad proudly told him, "My son's band The Hi-Fi's, were on the show"."They were pretty good", said his friend. Suddenly, I had credibility with my Dad. Up to that point, I'm sure he thought I should have a proper job.

Back to the gig at Lyons. JIMMY SAVILLE was compère. Along with us were The Honeycombs (another Joe Meek band who had a hit with "Have I The Right"), and top of the bill, the great DICK EMERY. Jimmy, as extrovert as ever, had his hair dyed like a black & white chequer board! He always had to be different from everyone else on the planet. He was a really crazy bloke and a bit of an odd-ball who lived for his music. Nobody knew then what was to come out about him in later years. I'll just leave it at that.

Both us, The Hi-Fi's and The Honeycombs, went down very well. They did a 45 minute spot and we played for dancing.

Dick Emery was still building his name at that stage but you could see that he was destined for stardom. He just had what it takes. He didn't have his own TV show then but he was well known for guesting on other people's shows.

Dick had a great operatic singing voice and he was doing voice-overs for commercials. As part of his act, he split the audience into four and got the first section to sing DI ESS. The second to sing O SYMEEN. The third APIMO and finally the fourth TORINGA.He got them all to practice their bits and when he put them all together, what did he get? DI ESS O SYMEEN APIMO TORINGA or THE ESSO SIGN MEANS HAPPY MOTORING!

One of the commercials that he had done the voice-over for at the time. Clever Eh?

Around this time, we were asked to arrange and record a song written by Valerie Avon of THE AVONS. A brother, sister & cousin vocal group. The song was called, "It's Gonna Storm". A really nice ballad. Anyway we had the song ready and we were told to go along to Abbey Road. The song wasn't for us and we didn't know who it was for. So we set up and played it. In the gallery was BILLY FURY. The song was for him apparently. After we'd played it through, he left the gallery without speaking to us. So he didn't like the song. That wasn't our fault but we did think it was a bit rude of him.

The Hi-Fi's, appeared on the Rediffusion TV show *Five O'clock Club*, recorded at the ITV Wembley Studios on November 17th '64.

Also on the show were TOMMY QUICKLY and The REMO 4 and HEINZ who used to be the Bass player in The Tornados. My overriding memory of the show was presenter MURIEL YOUNG standing, talking to hand puppets Fred Barker and Ollie Beak. One operated by WALLY WHYTON, yes the same Wally from The Vipers Skiffle Group, with a big smile on her face, probably because Wally had one hand inside Ollie Beak and his other hand up the back of her skirt on her bottom! These were such innocent times and full of fun and frolics.

We did another *KATHY KIRBY SHOW* because I like to think that Kathy liked us. On the bill this time was ADAM FAITH. At the risk of sounding boring, he was a really nice bloke too, with a wicked sense of humour. Also the show had a little South American Pianist called PEPE JARAMILLO. He was a bit like the Semprini or Peter Nero of South America so he could play a bit too!

Muriel Young

The show's star choreographer PETER GORDENO wanted
us to dance in the finale but that wasn't such a good idea.
But we ended up as Military Bandsmen with brass
instruments, on a pukka bandstand singing Alexander's
Ragtime Band. The Hi-Fi's, in those uniforms, pre-dated
The Beatles *Sergeant Pepper's Lonely Hearts Club Band* by a
long way. We visited the famous BERMANS COSTUMIER
in Soho to be fitted. Now that really is a place to behold!
Absolutely amazing! I've never seen so many different

outfits anywhere in my life. A brilliant experience.

Five o'clock club badge

Chapter 8   Backing Artists

We did quite a lot of backing work with the Hi-Fi's. Like KATHY KIRBY, Rock'n'Roll artists like VINCE EAGER, who was a diamond geezer, to the very beautiful JULIE ROGERS, ("The Wedding") with whom we spent an few weeks with as her band, augmented by her husband TEDDY FOSTER.

We played a great show at Woolwich Granada with JULIE. She shared top billing with THE ROCKIN'BERRIES. ("He's In Town" & "A Poor Man's Son)" THE PRETTY THINGS were next on the bill. They had Mick Taylor who later joined The Rolling Stones. Followed by THE SORROWS ("Take A Heart") and bottom of the bill, in print just bigger than the company who printed the poster, were TOM JONES & THE SQUIRES. They tore the place up! The audience went mad for Tom. All dressed in black leather trousers, black shirts and waistcoats, plus Cuban heeled boots. They just ROCKED! It was pretty obvious that TOM was going places from that moment.

Julie Rogers – To Malcom – love Julie

Another gig with Julie was at The Kursaal Amusement Park at Southend. The resident Big-band asked if we were all members of the Musician Union which we were not. So they threatened to walk off the stage. We had to take application forms from the rep before they'd let us play.

Tom Jones singing "Chills and Fever" on The Beat Room Show as he did on The Julie Rogers Show

We appeared on BBC2's show called *The Beat Room* and topping the bill was STEVIE WONDER. TOM JONES was on it too, backed by his band The Squires. Tom sang a rip-roaring version of "Chills And Fever." It was one of those shows where the audience danced around the artists who were set up about five feet high on sort of box-like podiums. STEVIE was really rocking and got up from his piano stool and started to dance. One of his singers just got to him in time before he took a dive into the crowd without meaning to. TOM was on fantastic form as usual.

We played somewhere in the Midlands on the same bill as TOMMY BRUCE. Now I've been nervous in my lifetime but I've never seen anyone as nervous as Tommy. I don't know why, because he was really good. The lead guitarist in Tommy's band, The Bruisers, was PETER LEE STIRLING. He's the guy who became DANIEL BOONE, and had a massive hit with "Beautiful Sunday" later on.

We also did a ten day tour of the UK backing CLARENCE Frogman HENRY. The Frogman bit has nothing to do with underwater swimming, before you ask. Clarence did a unique impression of a frog on his record "Ain't Got No Home". His best-known hit record in the UK was ("I Don't Know Why I love You,) But I Do". He was a really funny guy and we all thought, What the Hell are four South London young lads, still wet behind the ears, doing backing a Major American Rhythm & Blues singer? Well it didn't matter, we loved him and we like to think he liked

us. We played some all Black clubs, like The Marquee &
Tiles in London, where we thought we might have
problems but Clarence was right there with us all the way.
The poor bugger had a nasty touch of the "Chalfonts or
Farmers" whatever you like to call it and what made it
worse for him was that his promoter didn't give him a car
with a chauffeur.

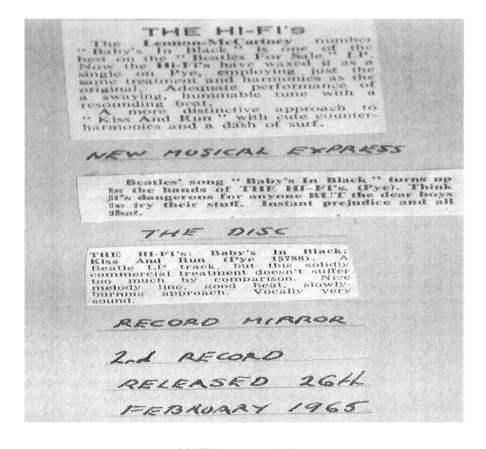

Hi-Fi's press cuttings

He just left Clarence to travel with us in our Commer one Ton van! It was so uncomfortable for him that he used to travel, sitting on a rubber inner-tube from a Lambretta scooter tyre, with his eyes watering. We did a really rockin' song of his called "Tore Up" and, for some reason I could never remember what key it was in. When his tour finished, he wrote me a personal autograph, which said, Best Wishes Malcolm. Clarence Frogman Henry, "Tore Up" is in Bb Cheers.

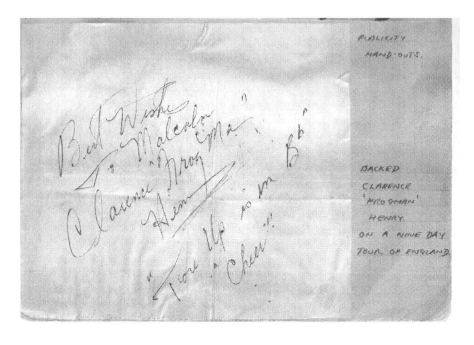

Clarence 'Frogman' Henry autograph and comment

We had a load of publicity photos taken by the

photographer of all the pop stars DEZO HOFFMAN. He'd taken THE PACKABEATS pictures too before. These were in Battersea Park at some ungodly hour of the morning so we'd be left alone. Who am I kidding! We weren't exactly The Beatles, so we weren't gonna get mobbed were we? It was freezing and Dezo even pushed us out in a boat on the lake to add to the effect.

The Hi-Fi's on Battersea Park Boating Lake
on a freezing morning publicity photo

Chapter 9 A Summer Season On The S.S. *Sooty*

Those photos at least got us an audition to go to Jersey, in the Channel Islands, for a summer season. We did five and a half months from early April to mid September travelling backwards and forwards to France, on a boat that used to be a tender for the Southampton liners, like the *Queen Mary* & *Queen Elizabeth 1*. It could only carry 550 passengers and some cars on the upper deck. We played in the lounge on the main deck. It was called *La Duchesse De Normandie*. We called her *The* S.S. *SOOTY*. That was because she used to emit immense clouds of smoke from her stack and sprinkle soot on anyone who was on the top deck in the open. She was owned by an Indian Entrepreneur, who went by the name of Noshirwan Fakaji Cowersgee (I think that's how you spell it). Of course, he was known to us all as Nosher.

Mainly, *Sooty* would travel to St Malo, four times a week and in between we'd go to Granville or Paimpol.

On board La Duchesse de Normandie ("Sooty")

All three were very pretty towns. The thing was, because the season started so early, the weather wasn't good and we had some really scary storms to contend with. We were booked to play on the return journeys only. So we had a lot of spare time to ourselves. We became good mates with the crew and we had a great laugh at some of the antics of the

Scouser deckhands. Two of them, who I can only remember as Fagin & Brady, used to have us in stitches. They would shout out, "HEY!" To the French quayside crew, and when they looked round, the scousers would sing, "MISTER TAMBOURINE MAN, PLAY A SONG FOR ME". It used to drive them Froggies nuts. They also used to sing "Black is the colour of our cat's arse" to the tune written by DONOVAN called "Colours".

On one trip from St Malo to Jersey, we were full of French people. The weather was awful! Blowing a force nine gale, I swear. The First Mate, Dusty Miller, sent Fagin & Brady down to the deck outside where we were supposed to be playing but we couldn't stand up let alone play. They were sent to calm the dear Frenchies so what did they do? They uncovered a lifeboat, put on life-jackets and sat in the boat singing "Abide with Me". Priceless.

In another massive gale, Brady was sent to the bridge with tea for the Captain, First Mate and Helmsman. He got to the top of the steep steps without spilling a drop. No mean feat. He had to slide the door open to get into the wheelhouse and as he did, he stepped in, the other side was open, she ship lurched to one side, he ran across the wheelhouse and threw the lot, tray and all into the sea! You couldn't write this stuff if you tried! It's often said, there's nothing funnier than life itself.

As the season gathered momentum, we were becoming well known on the Island. We played for The Battle of Flowers introduced by LESLIE CROWTHER a nice bloke but a bit too near the knuckle for some of the natives. We did some TV from the lovely Channel TV ITV studio where the staff we just great. I was to talk to some of them much later in my career after I had moved into Television.

There was a proper Night Club on the 5 Mile Beach, St. Ouens Bay called The Watersplash where you could get a nice meal, see a cabaret and have a dance to a band. We played there quite a few times when we weren't required to play on board ship. The popular singer who had hits in the '50s, DICKIE VALENTINE came to The Watersplash and we were booked to back him. He was great! A real professional, and master of his craft. BIG voice BIG personality and a damned fine comedian.

Dickie Valentine was an Ace performer in every way and we wished we could have had Red Price in The Hi-Fi's all the time!

Dickie Valentine

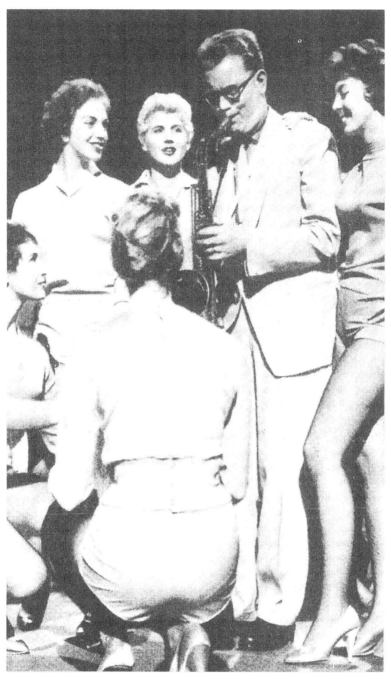

Red Price

We were in first rehearsal with Dickie, when an extra musician turned up. It was the brilliant RED PRICE. Tenor Sax player from Lord Rockinham's XI from the *Oh Boy!* TV show. What a nutter, but what a musician. I wish we could've had Red in the band all the time but he was only booked for the five day engagement.

A bit later we had to back DANNY WILLIAMS of "Moon River" fame. Danny was a good singer but I think he had a few other problems going on somewhere in his life that we don't need to talk about. We got through the shows without too much trouble anyway.

A double act of MALCOLM VAUGHN & KENNETH EARLE also came to the nightclub and we backed them as well. Malcolm went on to have hit records as a solo singer but I don't know what happened to Kenneth. I believe he became a very successful theatrical agent.

One lunatic memory of La Duchesse was, on a special day in the calendar of Jersey, the Governor of the island was to make a visit to the ship. It was a beautiful day but we were set up to play, as usual, in the lounge. It would have been better if we could have played on the upper deck outside. The thing was, we had to have a special generator to power our equipment. At a given signal from a crew member, we had to begin to play "God Save The Queen" as the Governor came up the gang-plank. We got the signal, off we went, God – Save – Our - BOOOOOM! The generator didn't want any part of this and blew up, filling the surrounding area with smoke. We couldn't play without power so that was that. After the Governor had left the ship, dear old Nosher came out with the priceless statement, "Well Brian, it might have been a loose wire!"

Imagine that, said in a Peter Sellers or Spike Milligan Indian voice and you're gone.

One weekend, we were booked to play in Paimpol at The Mayors banquet. That would have been great only we were invited to the banquet too! It was about a nine course meal and then we had to play. I would rather have gone to sleep for a couple of hours.

In Granville, we had a Citroen Safari complete with driver hired for us. He couldn't speak any English so guess who got stuck sitting in the front with him? Yep. Me. That's when my school French came into it's own. We had a long involved conversation and I didn't understand any of it.

It was only my second time in a casino, since Douglas I.O.Man. We set up the gear and I went upstairs for a gamble. In the old days of Francs, I was winning a few hundred, when I had to stop to go and play. Now the rule is, Quit when you're winning. Not me. I went back after playing and…….. lost the lot! I've been in several casinos since then but never gambled. I'm just not lucky that way.

How about this! The Hi-Fi's Orchestra with only 4 musicians?

We were booked to play on the tiny Channel Island of Sark, to commemorate the Fourth Centenary of the family who owned/governed the island. Getting onto the island was going to be interesting to say the least! *Sooty* was too big to get into their tiny harbour so we had to be ferried by smaller boat. A rowing boat! The fun started when they sent their Pilot out to guide S.S.*Sooty* in as close as possible. There was quite a swell on the sea and when the Pilot boat came alongside, he missed his footing and fell into the sea. One of the deckies threw a life-belt to him and the boat went round and picked him up. Looking very embarrassed, as he was soaked to the skin. When the rowing boat came to get us, we were convinced that all of our instruments were destined for Davy Jones' Locker. It took three trips back and forth to get it all on land much to our relief.

The Dame of Sark was a lovely, elegant and classy Lady. The dance was a brilliant success and they really looked after us well. After we'd finished playing, we had a couple of drinks. Well, a few more than a couple really. When it came to getting to the hotel at the other end of the island where we were staying, it was pitch black. Of course there are no street lights. No streets actually. No cars. Only bikes and no one was in a fit state to ride a bike. So, we walked the cliff-edge pathway lit by a nearby lighthouse. I kid you not! At one stage, Wrighty was walking along, gingerly touching the electric fence that kept the island sheep away from the cliff edge. It was only low voltage but he wouldn't have felt it anyway in his condition.

We came back to Jersey very late one night after taking the Frenchies home and some of us were a little worse for wear. We'd had one or two. When we pulled alongside the quay the intercom from the bridge called the deck-hand on the aft-end winch. We looked around and there he was, sleeping peacefully on the deck outside the galley, completely out of it! Wrighty and I answered the bridge, with a disguised voice, caught the rope that was thrown from the quayside, started the steam winch and pulled the ship alongside, tying her up beautifully. The guy on the quay-side looked at us and said, "Aren't you guys in the band?" We put fingers to lips and said, "Shhhhhhhh". And walked quickly away. We had a great summer. I look back fondly at everything that we did. Brian even met Paula, the lady who was to become his wife the following year so that was the icing on the cake.

Chapter 10   Changes, Changes And Off To Germany!

When we got home from Jersey, we didn't have much work and Ted decided to call it a day and quit the band. I phoned GARY UNWIN, the old PACKABEATS bassist and asked him to join us. He said he would if he could bring his friend MICKEY DOUGLAS with him. Mickey had played with CHRIS ANDREWS, LITTLE RICHARD and THE ROULETTES just to name a few. So nothing ventured etc., Gary & Mickey became Hi-Fi's and we became a five-piece. We even changed our name to FIVE'S A CROWD.

That didn't last five minutes as a name and we reverted back to The Hi-Fi's as it was a bit of a known name on the scene at the time.

We were also given a couple of songs to record by BUNNY LEWIS from Phillips/Fontana Records. One was written by ROGER COOK & ROGER GREENAWAY the other, a demo by GENE PITNEY and another by ERNI MARESCA.

Malcolm Lenny

Publicity Pic for possible name change to "Five's A Crowd"

COOK & GREENAWAY were having hit records with THE FORTUNES ("You've Got Your Troubles" etc.) and it was a good song called "Heaven Knows".

We also chose PITNEY'S song "I'm Not Ready For You Yet". ERNI MARESCA's big hit was "Shout, Shout, Knock Yourself Out" but his song "You're What's Happening Baby" just wasn't right for us. We recorded at the Phillips/Fontana Studio at Stanhope Gate in West London. I wasn't very well that day and kept throwing up into a waste-paper basket between takes. At one stage, Mickey had to sing with a plastic bucket on his head so that we couldn't see him straining to hit a high note. He was making us laugh so much it's a wonder we ever got it done. However Brian & I made a good job of "Heaven Knows" and I sang the lead voice on "I'm Not Ready For You Yet". We loved them. They were some of the best things that I personally have ever done.

Needing to get some experience together as a band we took a six week contract from the beginning of November in Konstanz (Constance) on the German/Swiss border. Konstanz was a stunningly beautiful town and we stayed in a Weinstube (Pub) overlooking the lake itself. It was like constantly (sorry for the pun) looking at a postcard.

We knew we didn't have enough material for the six hours we would be expected to play in Germany so we practised all the way there in the van. Driving through the Black Forest was a brilliant experience after the Autobahns across Belgium where all we could feel for hundreds of miles was the constant *Ker-Dunk, Ker-Dunk, Ker-Dunk, Ker-Dunk,* of the roads built by the Nazis during the war. They were made from concrete sections with gaps left for expansion in hot weather. That's why it went *Ker-Dunk* all the time! When we got to the Black Forest, it was late evening so it was dark. Suddenly a massive stag came out of the trees and ran straight into the side of the van with a really solid *BOINGGGG!* It hardly noticed us. It just shook its head and walked off into the trees again. We, on the other hand, had a dent in the side like something out of a *Tom & Jerry* cartoon! Vans had to be tough back then.

We were learning great Beach Boys and Four Seasons songs on the journey. I had a strong falsetto voice in those days and after the first night I couldn't speak let alone sing! Now John Lennon always said you had to have what he called Hamburg Throat, to perform in Germany. Well, he was right!

Some sort of voice started to appear after a week and we were off. Mickey had been great. Roaring his way through all the old Rock'n'Roll stuff that everybody knew all over the world. The town liked us so much that we were inducted in a Guild of Merchantmen called, THE ELEFANTEN and given a medallion to wear. I thought that was a lovely gesture and a great honour. If I ever get back to Konstanz, I shall wear my medallion with pride and go to visit the guild.

The German girls and guys loved us. I was a bit slow as far as girls went until one night I was packing up my guitar when a soft, sultry voice said, "Don't you go with girls?" I looked up and this vision of loveliness was there. Tall, blonde, blue eyes, the lot! She thought I was Gay! It wasn't called that then but you know what I mean. She was beautiful and I wasn't Gay. 'Nuff said.

She took me around and showed me the town, the lake, the Rheinfall at Schaffhausen. It was November and on one day, we had all four seasons in one. Sunshine, rain, howling wind and then six inches of snow! It was a magical day. I even met her family who thought I was not bad for a guitar-playing Englishman. I have to say at this point that I was promised to another, back home in England. When we got back to England, we had a good band but no work. So Phillips/Fontana wouldn't release our record. We were mortified. We had another offer to go back to Germany, so that's what we did. It was now January 1966.

My medallion from Konstanz The writing reads: "
That month we were made Honorary Members of the town guild of Merchants called The Elefanten"

Chapter 11   1966 And All That!

We played a few four week bookings in Mannehiem, Duisburg, Monchengladbach, Wuppertahl, Krefeld for example. We also began playing at The British army Headquarters, Rheindalen in the various officers mess's. All for pretty good money for the time.

We came back home to England in May because Brian and I had a long-standing booking that we had to honour.

June 4 '66 was the day I got married to Valerie, the girl I'd known since she was 16 and I was 18. She was now 21 and I was 23. Brian married Paula on the same day funnily enough, and then we returned to Germany taking our wives with us because we'd been offered a nice little earner in Mannehiem, in The Rheinland.

We moved on from there to another town called Duisburg. The club was called Tante Olga's literally translated as Auntie Olga's. Now Tante Olga was a formidable lady who scared the pants of us on first impression but she grew to love us as we did her. Well, she would because we were packing 'em in every night at the club. This was happening mainly because, as Mickey would say, we used to loon about and make the kids laugh. They never knew what we were going to do next, but then neither did we half of the time!

We returned yet again to Monchengladbach simply because we liked it there and they liked us. I had a few local friends there. One was the local barber named Gunther Wimmers who helped me a lot with learning to speak German. You know what it's like in barber shops, you talk sport, women, travel etc. Another guy, Eric "Long" Coumans, he was very tall hence the nick-name, was a bass-player in the local band The Shantanes. He had a mate called Lutz, I can't remember his surname but these guys became disciples of The Hi-Fi's, following us everywhere and spreading the word.

I rented a little farm cottage nearby in a village called Koch (pronounced Cock!) right opposite the British Army HQ. at Rheindalen. Ideal for a bit of English speaking shopping in the NAFFI. You could get a bottle of goodish brandy for about two pounds!

We worked at the great little club called The Derby Club. It was all done out like a stable inside. We loved it and the kids loved us. The owner, Herr Kupferberg, was a victim of the Nazi concentration camps and showed us what he called his telephone number, tattooed up his forearm. He held no grudges and was just happy to be making money out of the local teenagers.

One night, there had been a European Cup football match where Monchengladbach played host to Leicester City. I've no idea who won but the Leicester team came into the club that night. There was the England goalkeeper GORDON BANKS soon to become even more famous later that year by winning the World Cup at Wembley! PETER RODRIGUES the Welsh Captain, DAVID NISH soon to become another England international and PETER SHILTON who was Leicester's reserve goalie! I do remember how big Peter was.

What a night we had! We played our socks off. The team danced with the local girls and supped a few beers. We joined them afterwards for a few more and then went out into the car park for a kick-about. Now I'm not one to brag but I SCORED A GOAL AGAINST GORDON BANKS!!! O.K. so it was in the car park and the posts were only coats on the ground and he'd had a couple of beers but Hey, give me a break. Not many guitarists can say that, can they?

Leicester football players in club

We were in Krefeld, still in central Germany, when the

World Cup happened. We weren't always able to watch many games because we were working but when it came to the final, boy did we have a time! The Boss, Herr Munz, let us, our wives, three Italian waiters, four German waiters and his family, all crush into his lounge in front of his 24 Black & White TV set. Believe me the atmosphere was like being at Wembley! They Scored. The Germans went mad. We scored. We went mad and so on. The third goal? Don't even talk about it! Thank God for GEOFF HURST and the fourth goal.

D'you know, if I had a German Mark for every time I had to say, OK the third goal possibly wasn't a goal BUT the fourth one WAS! I could have bought a top-of-the-range BMW cash!

We heard down the grapevine that PAUL RAVEN, who was later to become GARY GLITTER, went on the stage of The Star Club Hamburg, in England football kit! Now that took some courage don't you think?

Leicester players autographs

Chapter 12   Hamburg

Now everyone has heard about British bands going to Hamburg. From The Beatles and most of the other Liverpool bands, to London bands and some of the big names of rock'n'roll from the U.S.A. Like, Ray Charles, Little Richard, Jerry Lee Lewis etc. It was an important piece of any band's CV to say they'd been to Hamburg.

We first went to play in a great little club in a sub-district called Barmbeck. It was about as far from the city centre as Morden is on the Northern Line to the West End of London. It was called The Big Apple strangely enough and it was owned by a great guy called Serge whose claim to fame was, that he had been the Chief Engineer on the ship *Exodus*. That's the ship involved in transporting Jewish people to form the State of Israel back in 1948.

We took over on New Years Eve from a very grubby English band whose personal freshness had a lot to be desired! The flat where we were going to stay was disgusting! So filthy that we couldn't believe it. Mattresses on the floor. Rubbish strewn all over the place. We cleaned it up as best we could but within two days, we were scratching!

We told Serge, we were off, unless he got us somewhere else to stay. So he emptied the flat above the club, decorated it throughout, bought new bunk-beds etc. We got the impression that we were good for business and he wanted us to stay.

Living there was great but we were still scratching. So someone went to the chemist to get some stuff that would fix the problem. It fixed the problem alright! The screams must have been heard for miles! We all used the stuff to get rid of the little buggers that were bothering us but it almost set your vitals on fire!

After the treatment, some of us were sitting on the top bunk-beds, examining our nether regions in close detail when the U-Bahn train stopped right outside our window. To see a train full of commuters, some strap-hanging, because it was so full, looking at some young guys butt-naked looking down at their groins must have been a sight to behold! Strangely enough, nothing was said about it. I fully expected to be featured on their equivalent of *News at 10* or the national newspapers but we didn't even get a visit from the local Constabulary!

Once again, the local kids loved us and we did a lot of things with them, on the days we had free time. Like, about ten carloads of us went to the nearest beach for the day. Did I say nearest? Timmendorferstrand was the nearest and that was on the Northern coast of the Baltic Sea. It took about two hours to get there and when we did, it was freezing! No one could take the risk of having a swim because the water was so cold the boys might have lost some bits of their anatomy.

There was a friend of Serge's who was a budding artist. His name was LORY. He was a completely bonkers Frenchman. He got up to his thighs and that was as far as he could manage. We sat on the beach, in the warm(ish) sun, drinking beer and wine. LORY and I had a face-pulling competition.

One thing sticks in my mind about the journey that day. On the way there, one side of the Autobahn was being re-surfaced for about ten miles. On the way back it had been finished and the other side was almost completed too!

Thinking of the time it takes to get anything done roadworks-wise in the UK, that was a real eye opener.

Face pulling with Lory, the mad Frenchman,
and on next page one of his paintings

Serge bought a brand new Mercedes 230SL sports car and took me for a spin round the Autobahn that circled Hamburg. My God did that thing shift! He scared the pants

off me because he wasn't a brilliant driver. When I say he scared the pants off me, I'm don't mean literally because I think I had filled them up after ten minutes!
Would you believe that Serge traded in the Merc for a Triumph TR3 which went even faster!

We challenged the local the local Barmbeck football team to an unofficial game at the local park. Our team was us, 5 Hi-Fi's, and six waiters and other staff from The Big Apple. It was hilarious. We lost 7-3 basically because we were ridiculously unfit which noticed mainly when I tried to get up onto the stage that night and could hardly bend my legs! Dear old Mel Wright score the goal of the century in that game. He was blind as a bat without his glasses so he wore them with an elastic band round the back of his head, holding them on. They were like milk bottle bottoms they were so thick. I think it was Mickey who crossed the ball, shouted, "On yer 'ead Mel!" Mel whipped off his glasses, the ball hit him fair and square in the face and straight in the goal! He never saw it but what a goal.

We got our own back when we challenged them to a ten-pin bowling match. Gary and I were pretty good at it and we murdered them.

A bunch of us went to The Top Ten Club in the city centre where TONY SHERIDAN was playing. Tony was the guy who The Beatles backed when they were out there a couple of years before. He was a good singer and a great guitarist. He was very well known in Germany and had lots of hit records.

Gary had gone with one of the waitresses from the Big Apple and we were all sitting having a beer, watching Tony when, out of the blue, a guy came up to Gary and said, "That's my girlfriend". It was the girl's ex-boyfriend who had had too many beers. He grabbed Gary from behind, pinning his arms by his sides. I grabbed the guy in the same way and a waiter grabbed me the same way too!

It must have looked hilarious with three blokes locked together in some sort of a Daisy Chain. Someone yelled, "That's the band from The Big Apple!" and they all let go.

It was all over in seconds and TONY SHERIDAN invited us up onto the stage to join him in a couple of numbers. It was magic! I thoroughly enjoyed myself and felt it was an honour to play with a guy who had played with The Beatles.

Soon after that, we were booked to play at the world famous STAR CLUB. To have trodden the boards where the likes of Ray Charles, Little Richard, Jerry Lee Lewis and of course THE BEATLES had been, was a great honour for any band. We were destined to play quite a lot at The Star Club and we built ourselves up a good fan-base very quickly. One day, the Boss Manfred Weissleder told us we needed to make some records. So he signed us up and put us in contact with Siggi Loch, who was the record producer for The Star Club record label.

Gary Unwin used to write songs. Mickey Douglas and Brian Bennett used to write songs together and I would add bits and pieces if anyone asked me! So the first single was Gary's song "I'm A Box" with the B side "No Two Ways" written by Mickey, Brian and Me. "I'm A Box" was an obscure song about a box who brought a bloke's birthday present to her and was then thrown away. Don't ask! It's redeeming factor was the vocal backing that went Mum-Mum-Mum. That was the bit that the Germans liked because they could sing it! "No Two Ways" was a bit like "Summer Holiday". A bit sing-a-long. It sold really well, so Siggi got us back in the studio to do a follow-up very quickly. Both written by Mickey & Brian, this one was called "Snakes & Ladders", a song likening a love affair to the board game. You know what I mean. "Up the ladders and down the snakes. It was backed with "Tread Softly For The Sleepers". Which came from our days of being woken up at some ungodly hour of the morning, when we lived above Tante Olga's club in Duisburg.

I have a wonderful memory of walking into the foyer of The Star Club before playing one evening and seeing the West German Hit Parade with us at number one and number four in the same week! Not many bands could boast that I bet?

The Star Club always had three bands at any one time so I got to meet loads of other musicians. Some well known, others destined to become big stars. There was a great Liverpool band called IAN and The ZODIACS who were well established in Germany.

 I became good mates with Ian Edwards and we used to go drinking together at The Blockhutte across the road from The Star Club. Arthur, Charlie and Freddie were the other guys. All great guys and respected musicians. We shared the bill with them and THE V.I.P.S, who were later to become SPOOKY TOOTH. They were a serious bunch of guys who played blues and that was that! They had a guy on organ who was fantastic and used to rock his organ around back & forth while he was playing. He became well known later as EMERSON, LAKE and PALMER. Yes it was KEITH EMERSON.

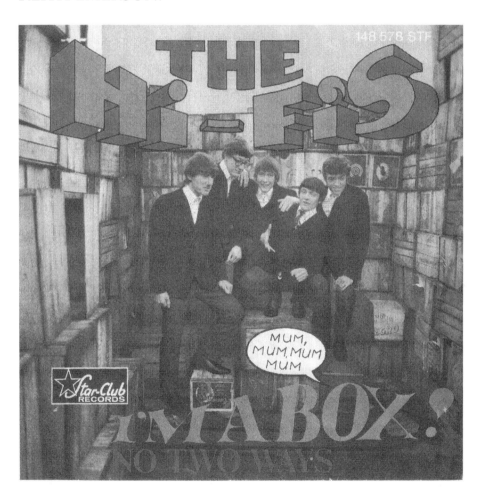

The Hi-Fi's No.1 Hit record in Germany '64

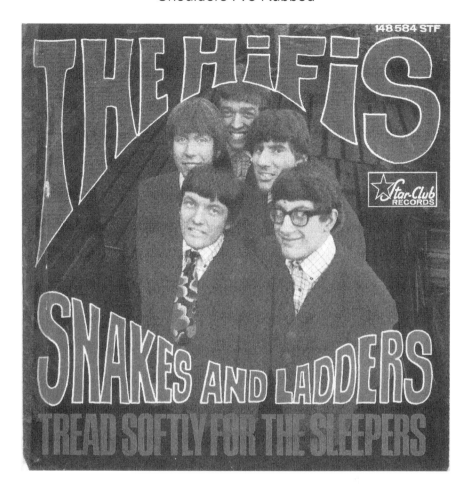

The Hi-Fi's No.4 Hit record in Germany

There was a really good girl band known as THE
LIVERBIRDS who had been in Germany for a long time
and had had a few hit records. Mary, the drummer, was
married to FRANK DORSTAL who sang lead for the best-
known German band THE RATTLES.

We were asked to sing backing vocals on stage behind GRAHAM BONNEY for his hit song "Supergirl". His band thought we sang the backing better than they did. Nice compliment.

There was a really good band called The King-Pins who's singer, Roy Grant, was the nearest thing I'd ever heard to Gene Pitney. Seriously, you could close your eyes and it was Gene! Roy even went bright red in the face when he hit the top note at the end of "I'm Gonna Be Strong". He became assistant stage manager of The Star Club a bit later on.

Ex-SEARCHER TONY JACKSON came to the club while we were there but he was having a few problems with drinking. His band, were not happy about it although it never seemed to affect Tony's actual performance. One afternoon when Tony was rehearsing, I saw two very familiar faces, sitting in one of the alcoves beside the dance floor watching Tony rehearse. One was Tony's old buddy, ex- SEARCHERS drummer CHRIS CURTIS. The other was none other than BRIAN EPSTEIN! The odd thing was that they were sitting a little too close for comfort if you know what I mean.

We actually topped the bill when the other two bands were THE PRINCES Of ISRAEL and THE DOLLIES with The Mixture. All nice people but we had the following from the crowd so I suppose we warranted top billing.

THE BOSTON SHOWBAND with singer PAUL RAVEN, came for a couple of weeks and they were the nucleus of what was to become GARY GLITTER and THE GLITTER BAND.

Paul was always <u>very showbiz</u> and some of the other bands used to laugh at him but he didn't care one bit. He always gave a top-notch performance. A born show-off if ever there was one but good fun to be around. There was no suggestion of what was going to happen with Paul in later years. He was just very eccentric.

Wrighty and I became drinking buddies with Paul and more than once we would have to assist him in getting back to his room in The Pacific Hotel where all the bands used to stay as part of their contract. That hotel was a den of iniquity and a hot-bed of risqué behaviour. Once again, 'nuff said.

THE BOSTON SHOWBAND used to do their own spot

before introducing Paul and they were pretty good. Irish Showbands were always made up of good quality musicians. One day, they asked us to sing backing vocals on their recording of "I Believe". They did us the return favour of playing Brass on one of our LP tracks, "Up And Over".

Whenever a band was playing their last night at the club, all the other bands would go on-stage with them for their last number. When it was time for Paul Raven and The Boston Showband to leave, Mel Wright went on with their drummer. Gary Unwin made it two basses, Brian Bennett added his organ and Mickey & I borrowed a brass instrument. He had a sax and I had a trumpet. What a band! We played "Land Of A Thousand Dances" which was fine for me because I only had to play 1 note all the way through.

I like to think that Wrighty adding an extra drummer to the band was the blueprint for THE GLITTER BAND's future. They had two drummers on their first hit "Rock'n'Roll Part 1".

Another time at the club, we were on with THE REMO 4. A brilliant band, which included TONY ASHTON on keyboards. Tony formed ASHTON, GARDENER & DYKE a few years later and had a big hit with "Resurrection Shuffle". The Hi-Fi's and THE REMO 4 became good mates for a while when we were working together.

Other top Liverpool bands who played at the same time as us were, King-Size Taylor and The Dominos, Lee Curtis and the Allstars. A great singer who fronted The Undertakers was Jackie Lomax. Ian Edwards from Ian and The Zodiacs became a real good mate. They were a real 'tasty' band who appealed to the blokes, 'cos they knew how to play rock'n'roll!

On one occasion, an almost unknown band was booked to do two nights only. They were called THE JIMI HENDRIX EXPERIENCE.

They were due on straight after us. I was standing with our drummer MEL, at the bar at the back of the club. The curtains opened to a very dark stage. There was a strange noise that sounded like something was feeding back. Where was the stage manager? I started to run down the aisle to help.

Suddenly, all hell broke loose to the song "Foxy Lady"

Jimi Hendrix at The Star Club Hambu

I'd never heard anything like it! For 45 minutes I was mesmerised. Nothing was miked up but, by God, it was powerful! Jimi had two Vox AC30 amps and Noel Redding had twoVox bass amps. No Marshalls around at that time.

The next day, I went to the club during the afternoon to fix a problem with one of my guitars. I could hear someone playing an acoustic guitar in the next dressing room. That's a bit tasty, I thought. I pushed open the door and there was Jimi. I just had to tell him what I thought of the previous night's performance. He said a very quiet, Thank you and invited me in along with my 12 string. I sat down, we chatted, we jammed a bit. I let him play lead, naturally. And that was that. I didn't know what he would become later. There are no photographs to prove it happened but I know it did. He's dead and I'm still here and still playing at 74. It's a great memory and it's all mine. You should see the youngsters faces when I tell them.

During one of our times playing at The Star Club, Alan Clarke from The Hollies was in Hamburg doing a show on TV and he came to the club to see us. He remembered the name of the band from the tour we did with them a while before. He bought that great American singer DEL

SHANNON with him. They watched our first set and then we all went together for a beer in The Beer Shop next door. It was pretty special to be chatting with such a big star from the States. I'm sure that every band must have played Del's "Runaway" at some time in their lives.

Del Shannon . . . .

When we had to go back on to do another set, Alan & Del went off to find some "action" in another bar down the street. We met up with Alan later on, back in The Beer Shop. He told us Del had gone back to his hotel with a very red face! Apparently, they had gone into another bar, which had curtained off alcoves. They each bought a bottle of Deutsche Sect, which is like champagne only cheaper and selected a girl to drink it with. After about five minutes, there was a yell from Del! He said he'd put his hand up her kilt and found a set of male bits & pieces! They both quit the bar at 100mph with Alan laughing at Del's shocked expression.

Grosse Freiheit was always an interesting place and I'm sure it could cater for anyone's likes and desires. For some reason, George, the Star Club doorman, regarded me as a special guy. We used to have a beer together and although he didn't speak English, we had some great conversations. His picture is in the book of The Star Club and it's the same picture as he gave me when we left the club. He signed it, To my best friend Malc. The best man of lead guitar. Many Greetings.

The Hi-Fi's have got a couple of photos in The Star Club

book too. It's amazing to be in the same book as so many really big stars of Rock'n'Roll and some of the biggest names in the world of pop music.

Dates from Star Club billings
featuring HI-FI's and Jimi Hendrix

We made an album titled *SNAKES & HI-FI*'s at Cologne University. It wasn't a live album but we set up on the stage in the concert hall, without any audience and played as if live and the engineers recorded us as we played. This was a good bit different from being squashed into Joe Meek's front room or the very professional studios at Abbey Road. It was a real mixture of songs, all self-written except one called "Here I Stand". This was our version of a Rip Chords record where I showed off my, shriekingly high, falsetto voice.

My favourite memory of the session was a song written by Gary Unwin called "You're Haunting Me". Gary sang it and played classical guitar. Brian Bennett played the concert hall pipe organ and I got down on my knees, underneath

Brian and played the bass notes on the foot pedals. He put labels on the notes so I knew which ones to play. Brian was a great organist but expecting him to play the foot pedals as well was just not on! With a Beach Boys-style vocal break in the middle, it wasn't a half-bad song.That album has been seen up on e-bay for £300-£400!

While we were in Cologne, a massive package tour came to the city. Our mates, Ian and The Zodiacs were on the bill,

The Hi-Fi's one-and-only LP on The Star Club label

so we went to see it. I can't remember who topped the bill ˙
but it had THE KINKS, DAVE DEE, DOZY, BEAKY, MICK
& TITCH, THE SPENCER DAVIS GROUP, PINK FLOYD ˙
to name but a few! The Kinks and Spencer Davis were
brilliant as expected. Dave Dee & Co were very big at the
time in Germany but Pink Floyd? Oh dear!

When the curtains opened, they were standing with backs

to the audience, all with cigarettes, either in their mouths or stuck in the head-stock of their guitars and LOUD! My God, it was so obvious that they didn't want to be there. They were so wrong for that tour but that's how the promoter had put it together.

After the show, we went back to their hotel for a beer with Ian & he boys and as I walked into the reception area, I saw the brilliant STEVIE WINWOOD leaning against the wall beside the lift, with a lunatic grin on his face. He slowly slid down the wall into a crumpled heap and went to sleep. I think he'd had just one too many bottles of fizzy lemonade. He was only 17 at the time, so he's excused.

Stevie is one of my all-time favourite singers/organists/ guitarists and "Stevie's Blues" is one of my all-time favourite B sides.

A post script to The Star Club Hamburg. 99% of all the guys and girls who played at the club all became mates while you played there. Anybody who was "too big for their boots" was quickly brought down to size or they spent a very lonely time there.

Nuff Said!

Chapter 13   Fatherhood!

My wife shocked me with the news that she was pregnant. Right out of the blue. Well, it was very cold in Germany and you had to do something to keep warm.

The baby was due to arrive in April/May '67 so I had to make a big decision. I had to give up the band and get an ordinary job or carry on touring. I had seen a few marriages fall by the wayside because the father was away working so I decided to pack it in and go back to England. That was a very hard decision to make and it almost broke my heart to leave but I just had to do it.

My last gig with The Hi-fi's was at the British Army HQ. Rheindalen, in the NCO's Mess. It was very emotional for all of us and when it was over we all went for a massive drink with some "squaddie" friends. One of them, John Maskell, was a chauffeur for one of the Senior Officers and he said I could sleep in their billet. Jeez, did we have a drink or what! Allegedly, I consumed about eight pints of

Double Diamond and then washed it all down with about eight large Brandies!

On the way back to the billet, I was being helped along by John and another soldier whose name escapes me. Walking was a bit of a problem at the time. We took a short-cut across the parade square. Unbeknown to me, personnel are not supposed to cross the square unless they're on parade.

Well, we're half way across, doing the Glasgow two-step, that's two forward and one back, when up pop two red-caps with torches! "Halt! Who goes there?" Both the lads, holding me up leap to attention, although they were in civvies and reeled off name, rank and number. I said, in my very best slurred English, "And I'm a F*****G Civilian".

"Get 'Im orf the square lads, and we'll say no more".

They "doubled" me off to the billet and nothing more was said.

In the morning, I was woken to the strains of a bugle, playing "Reveill"e, followed by The Beatles singing, "Let me take you down...... 'cos I'm going to..........Strawberry Fields". The lads had a record player synchronised to go off like an alarm clock.

How the hell I managed to eat a full English breakfast after all that alcohol, but I did, and then it was time to say goodbye to my great mates, The Hi-Fi's.

 MICKEY DOUGLAS, GARY UNWIN, BRIAN BENNETT and MALCOLM "MEL" WRIGHT. Great boys with whom I had a load of fun and I wouldn't have missed it for the world. We shook hands, hugged each other and they drove off on their long journey to Berlin where they were playing next. I just stood and cried for a while after I'd waved them out of sight. Then John took me, my Gibson 335ES TD, my Vox AC 30 amp & cab and my large suitcase to the railway station in Monchengladbach town centre.

It was a horrible journey, into the unknown really. Because all I'd ever wanted to do, was be a musician and now it was over.

After the long train journey and an awful crossing from the Hook of Holland to Harwich, I boarded another train to London and eventually got home to Balham where we were going to live with my parents until we could sort something out. It wasn't an ideal situation but we had no option.

My first daughter Jane was born at Annie McAll's Maternity Hospital at Stockwell, South London, on May 2nd 1967. It was very exciting for me to be a Dad at 24, two days before she was born.

Since I'd been home, I had looked for work that was connected with music. I didn't want to go back to the GPO engineering. That would have been an admission that I'd failed to make it in the music industry. I tried to get a job with dear old CHARLIE WATKINS, the man who now ran the successful company, Watkins Electric Music or WEM, to give it it's proper title. But there was nothing I could do that was any use to Charlie. Earlier on when I first began to play music, I had the second Watkins Copicat Echo that Charlie ever made.

It was a brilliant piece of kit and a heck of a lot cheaper that anything else that was around at the time. I lost it many years later when I was out in Germany.

I had three Lenny cousins who worked in the film business. They were all brothers. Jack was a carpenter who worked for Rediffusion Television at Wembley Studios. Bill was a free-lance feature film Editor and the youngest brother Tony, worked for The Andersons who used to make all the puppet shows for TV like *Stingray*, *Supercar* and *Thunderbirds* etc. as effects editor or music editor.

MUSIC EDITOR? My ears pricked up! Maybe I could get into something like that? I almost forgot to mention that Tony was Editor of The Beatles film *Yellow Submarine*. How about that then.

I 'phoned Bill and he invited me to Shepperton Studios where he was working at the time. It was a magical visit. Bill took me around and showed me cutting rooms, dubbing suites, studio floors, but the overriding memory was the set for *Oliver!* the musical. It was the Regency Crescent set for the song "Who will Buy, This Beautiful Morning". When you see the film, it's all very real, but the houses only had a front and the rest had platforms for people to stand on to lean out of the windows. No matter, it was a brilliant sight to someone who'd never seen a film set before.

Bill and I talked a lot and he told me that I couldn't get a job in the industry unless I had a union card. That's how it was in those days. The union was very strong and looked after their members.

He said I could use his name to get an interview but I would have to start right at the bottom in a film-processing laboratory. Bill had a good name already. One of his first jobs as an editor was BOB MONKHOUSE'S first film *Dentist In The Chair.* He went on to edit *Mackenna's Gold* starring GREGORY PECK and the first version of the JAMES BOND film *CASINO ROYALE* which starred David Niven, Peter Sellers, Ursula Andress, Woody Allen and Orson Wells! He worked for Hammer Films too and edited their version of *Dracula* starring Christopher Lee and Peter Cushing. So you can see, he had a bit of clout!

Chapter 14   Starting In The Film And Television Industry

I had an interview at George Humphries Laboratories in London where they processed feature film, documentaries, commercials etc. It was a bit of a weird place to work and my main concern was that everyone wore white dust coats, which was a throw-back to my days in the GPO Engineering where everyone wore brown dust coats or boiler suits. Still, I had to start somewhere and this was right at the bottom of a completely new career for me.

I spent the first six months getting old black & white film negatives housed in rusty old film cans, out of the vault. I used to have to get them cleaned chemically, before getting the printers to make copies. The guys who looked after the vault had a great sign above their door that said,

"YOU HAD IT, YOU LOOK FOR IT!"

That must have been for those people who took "negs" out without doing the necessary paperwork. It wasn't exactly a rewarding job but I had to be earning to support wife and baby and I knew I had to start at the bottom.

After those six months, I got a better-paid job as a viewer. Now that meant I had to watch a film or a documentary or a commercial to make sure it was technically and physically correct. Take it from me that when you've seen a film six times or a commercial twenty times, it gets a bit boring!

I did get to meet a man by the name of HARRISON MARKS. He was responsible for most of the nude films made in those days. I suppose they would be classed as "soft porn" today. He was a strange man but he did make me laugh one day when he was watching some rushes (that's raw, uncut film) and when there was a close-up of a young girl's pubes, he stopped the projector and said, "There's a hair in the gate".(That's the bit of the projector where the light shines through the film) Normally that would have been a single hair caught up in the printing process and the copy would have been rejected.

One of the funny things that happened while doing that job was that I was given sole charge of viewing dozens of copies of a certain film. That was called *Helga*.

I should explain that I was the only male viewer out of about eight to ten people. *Helga* was a foreign film about SEX EDUCATION! It wasn't the sex bit that the females didn't want to see, it was the giving birth bit that upset them all! Some of them even said it made them feel sick, watching a baby pop it's head out for a look round, before deciding if it wanted to stay or not.

It didn't worry me because I'd seen all the "naughty bits" when I was viewing all the HARRISON MARKS films.

I trundled along for a few more months before getting a job with the man who was responsible for handling all the bits of film and tele-recordings done by Thames Television. His name was Eddie Hill and he always gave the impression that he was on roller-skates, he used to move around the building so fast!

One day Eddie told me there was a job on offer at LONDON WEEKEND TELEVISION, who shared the seven day transmission with Thames TV. He said I should go for it because they were a new and ambitious company.

I applied and got the job!

LONDON WEEKEND TELEVISION was a new and

exciting company housed at the old Rediffusion Television Studios at Wembley, so living in Balham wasn't a good idea. Living with my parents wasn't easy and after about six months, we lived with my in-laws in Borehamwood, Hertfordshire. That was so we could get on to the local council house list. We did that by deliberately over-crowding their house. That wasn't really any easier in a lot of ways but at least it was closer to my new job. I bought a Raleigh Wisp moped. Well that's all I could afford at the time. Shortly afterwards, I up-graded to a Honda 90. (Bikers, eat your hearts out!)

Now I have to tell you an absolutely <u>true story</u> about my motorbike test. Living in Borehamwood, meant that the test centre was in Barnet, about four miles away. On the day of the test, I had completed all the moves and answered all the necessary questions so that only left the emergency stop test to do. So the Examiner told me to, "Go to the end of this road, turn right, turn right again at the end of that road, turn right again and come back into this road. When you do, I will step out with my clip-board and when you see me, bring your vehicle to a stop, in the safest and quickest way you can". "No problem", says I. Off I go up the road, turn right, turn right again and there is a massive furniture van completely blocking the road. So, I turn round and go back, turn right and head for the next road. Anyway, to cut a long story short, it must have taken almost ten minutes to get back to the Examiner. When I did, there's an ambulance there! The poor bugger had stepped out in front of the wrong Honda 90 and got knocked down! Barnet General Hospital was only two minutes away. That's how they got there so quickly.

Now, I related that story some years later to BOB HOLNESS & DOUGLAS CAMERON on their LBC Radio show one morning and they creased up! But the strange thing is that, some considerable time later, the very same situation appeared on an episode of *Some Mothers Do 'Ave 'Em* and Frank Spencer (alias Michael Crawford) did exactly what I did during his motorbike test. Someone must have heard my story don't you think?

The job I had at LWT, wasn't that exciting either really. I had to physically join together 2,000ft reels of different commercials to be transmitted between programmes. I only really worked half a day Wednesday and a full day Thursday & Friday. The stuff was transmitted Friday from 5.15 through to close down on Sunday night. Monday the three of us doing the job came in and took them all apart again ready to be put in a different order for the next weekend. Mind numbing stuff!

I had a lot of time when I had nothing to do so I used to wander into the studios and watch shows being recorded. Basically I was on the look-out for a job that I thought I could get into as soon as possible. I remember watching the great RONNIE CORBETT, working on a variety show where ENGLEBERT HUMPERDINCK was the guest star.

Well, Hump was a star! The trouble was that he needed everyone to know he was! He was looking round all the time to see which of the girls working on the show, fancied him most. A bit sickening. I'm delighted to say that in later years, Englebert seems to have become a really nice guy and he's worked hard and long for his success.

I used to sneak into the audience seats when STANLEY BAXTER was rehearsing for his top-rated comedy show. He was a very, funny, man and deserved all the accolades that he got. I missed the episode when HILDA BAKER had a bath full of some thing like porridge poured over her from the gantry above and the bath came loose and fell on her. I think she sued LWT for their back teeth after that but it looked very funny on screen.

On one of my wandering trips around the studios, I passed a small sound studio. The "Stand-By" light was on but not the "On-Air" one. I pushed open the door and heard the most beautiful music. It could only have been one of my most favourite musicians of all time, STEPHAN GRAPELLI! The way he played the violin was absolutely original. There will never be another to play like him.

He had someone on piano with him. I couldn't see who it was, so I sneaked round behind a curtain to see. It was only PETER NERO! Another world-class musician. Well, I just kept quiet and enjoyed their music for about 20 minutes, all to myself. They had no idea that I was there and I was totally on my own. I really wanted to go and speak to them but I didn't dare. These were internationally regarded musicians and I shouldn't have been there anyway.

Around this time, I lost my dear old Dad. I was on holiday down in Cornwall with my family and my in-laws. We'd been out for the day and on returning to the caravan site where we were staying I had a message to ring my sister. She asked if I was alone and then said, "There's no other was to say this but Dad died last night". I sank to the floor of the phone box in total shock and disbelief. Nothing like this had ever happened to me before. He was only 66.

Every time I listen to that wonderful song "The Living Years" by Mike and The Mechanics with Paul Carrack on lead vocal and he gets to the third verse where he sings the line, "I wasn't there that morning, my Father passed away", I'm in bits!

Because I can't remember telling my Dad that I loved him although I know I did. I like to think he did. He was a lovely bloke. Soft as putty and always first to the bar to buy his friends a drink even though he never had much money.

Chapter 15   Moving On

My wife was noticing that something was missing from my life. Well of course it was music!

She had seen an advert in the local paper saying,

Wanted: Guitarist/Vocalist for local band. Ring this number etc.

Well I rang the number and was told that auditions were being held at the Watford Top Rank Suite next Sunday. The suite was a big venue where they held Banquettes, Balls, Cabarets and the like.

So I turn up with my faithful old Gibson 335ES TD to find that I'm auditioner number 15. On the stage was the rhythm section of piano, bass and drums plus a tenor sax player. The guy doing the talking was a very smartly dressed Northern chap. His name was George Bradley and it was his dance band that we were auditioning for. Blimey! A dance band! This was going to be a challenge.

All the guys before me played something that a group of the day would've played. Nothing wrong with that but nobody stood out as any better than the rest. So now it's my turn and I'm last up.

I go up on the stage and the guys who've been playing all afternoon look well pissed off and bored to tears. "What are you gonna play?" says George. Thinking quickly, I reply, "How about "The Girl from Ipanema"?" Well the tenor player was out of his chair like a rocket! Hooking on his Sax as he moved. It was something different from everyone who'd gone before. I played it. I sang it. George asked me if I could play pop songs too. I said, "no problem". I got the job. Now, George used to tell me that he had taken JOHN BARRY'S place in The John Barry Seven when John left to write music for Bond films and I had no reason not to believe him.

It was a real learning curve for me to step out of a pop band into a dance band where everyone was a sight-reader, because I couldn't read music! Mind you, I was a very quick learner and I had a good ear. Plus I had a very good knowledge of chords and I could play in any key.

The funny thing about reading music surfaced almost a

year later. We were playing for the area, knock-out stage of the BBC original TV show, *Come Dancing.* We had to play very strict tempo tunes so that the competitors could strut their stuff.

George had a small metronome in his hand to make sure that we did all the tunes at exactly the right speed. It was a hard night for the band but we played very well. In the dressing room afterwards, George came over to me and asked, Why didn't you play the solo that's written in "Lady Is A Tramp" ? I replied, "Because I can't read music, George". "WHAT!!!" says George, "But you've been in the band for almost a year!" "Yes", I said, "And you hadn't noticed, had you?". Just then John Hibberd, the bass player, put up his hand and said, "Neither can I, George". George stood open mouthed until the sax player, Brian, said, "Leave 'em alone, George. They're good blokes and they add some natural Balls to the band."

George did leave us alone and I had two and a half years with him.

We used to work Wednesday/ Friday/ Saturday and Sunday and any extras on the other days when required. We had some characters in the band. Trevor the first trumpet could hit high notes akin to Maynard Ferguson from my Simon Dee show days. Tony, the trombonist was a serious guy who did all the bands arrangements and liked a drink or three.

The band used to set up on one half of a circular stage, which revolved. The rhythm section was on stage left and the saxes were on stage level with the trumpets raised up behind them and Tony sat at the top of the "pyramid" on his own. On one occasion, Tony had downed "a couple" and was a bit wobbly on his feet. We were playing a beautiful slow foxtrot called Laura which had a trombone solo in the middle.

Tony came down from his "perch" to the front and played a lovely, muted, solo. Then he turned round and walked back, up to his position at the top and fell straight through the curtains. I collapsed! I thought I was the only one to have seen him disappear. We played one more number and someone pushed the "tit" to turn the stage round for the DJ to do his bit for general dancing and there was Tony. Spark out lying across the DJ's speaker cabs! We got him off as quietly as we could and back to the dressing room.

The fault was probably George's anyway, because we used

to go across the road to the pub for a beer in our break and the rule was that when George called, "Time! Get Back on the Stage you lazy B******ds!" If you had anything left in your glass, even a quarter of an inch, you had a Triple 'A' Barley Wine stuck in it and you had to down it in one! I got caught a couple of times like that and only just got through the night.

I used to ride my motorbike from Borehamwood to Watford past the Aldenham Reservoir and it's a wonder I didn't end up in the water sometimes. There was no breathalyser in those days, luckily. Sometimes, I even rode my motorbike with my lovely Gibson guitar across the handlebars too! In it's case of course.

I met some stars who came to the Top Rank to do a cabaret spot. ROY CASTLE was one who stood out. A lovely bloke and very versatile. Funny, nice singing voice and the only man I saw who could get a tune out of an aluminium kettle. What a shame he died so young, thanks to passive smoking.

I've always hated smoking and since I nearly lost my Mum due to it, I'm even more adamant about it. Mum contracted some strain of pneumonia from being outside, sweeping snow off our pathway when she wasn't wearing warm enough clothing. They took her out of the door on a stretcher and her face was a dull grey colour. The Doctor at the hospital said, "Does she smoke?" I told him that she smoked ten un-tipped Players cigarettes every day.

Roy Castle at The Top Rank Suite Watford. Lovely Guy

He told me that if she didn't stop, she would be dead in five years! I told her that she doesn't smoke any more and if she did I would smack her! I was about 16 at the time. Mum was 56. She lasted another 30 years without smoking and finally died at 86.

171

BOB MONKHOUSE was another artist who stood out. What a professional! He had a mine of material to call on. He used to swap banter with the audience during his act and he'd keep going back to people he'd spoken to ten minutes before and he never got a single name wrong. We didn't need to back Bob musically because he brought it with him. He was the first person who came with a small case, like a brief case, with a piece of equipment in it, which he plugged into the PA system. It must have been just a tape recorder but it had all his backings for his songs and sound effects for some of his jokes. But the amazing thing was that once he started it and his act, it just ran with him. He never stopped it. Everything was timed to perfection and everything happened in the right place! Brilliant!

MR. ACKER BILK'S PARAMOUNT JAZZBAND came one Sunday to play. His banjo player was carrying his banjo in one hand and the case in the other. The reason for this? The case was full of Merrydown Cider. Well the band <u>was</u> from Somerset (Like Me!) He drank the whole lot, about four bottles before they went on and, believe it or not, he never missed a cue or played a "Bum Note". What a pro.

One of our replacements for our main vocalists turned out to be a young JOE FAGIN who went on to sing the theme tune to the TV show *As Time Goes By* starring Judy Dench and Geoffrey Palmer.

Joe also sang loads of the Jingles for BBC Radio. He was a really good singer and good fun to work with. He also sang the theme song to *Aufwiedersehen Pet* which became a massive Top Ten hit

I got to meet an absolute hero of mine, at The Top Rank, one evening. The Mighty GEOFF HURST! Scorer of a hat trick of goals in the 1966 World Cup Final at Wembley and part of the only England team ever likely to win the World Cup in my lifetime. He was doing a sponsored tour of venues to promote a new beer, whose name escapes me at the time of writing. Maybe a bit of a comedown for a man of his stature but, let's face it, everyone has to earn a crust where and when they can. Not like today's footballers who get obscene salaries, in my opinion. I told Geoff the story about the circumstances how I saw the game in Germany. He said he could imagine the excitement in that room above the club. He was a cracking geezer and I'm very pleased to say that I met him.

Geoff Hurst (What a Hero!)

The two and a half years I spent with The George Bradley Band really meant that I had two jobs at the same time. At least four nights a week in the band, plus my job at LWT. It was knackering!

During my wanderings at the TV studios, I became interested in the film editors who worked in the same part of the studios as I did. I used to stand in the doorway of their edit suite, watching what they did with admiration. If you remember, two of my cousins Bill and Tony Lenny were editors so maybe this was a way in? There were about eight editors. All different personalities. But the one who stood out was a guy by the name of ALAN RAVENSCROFT. It took a while before I realised that Alan was the brother of JOHN PEEL the BBC Radio Disc Jockey. Alan had the personality of a mountain! He had a label on his door that said,

ALAN RAVENSCROFT & RAY WEEDON

THEY MAKE IT HAPPEN!

(Ray was Alan's assistant editor.)

I'll always remember the day Alan came in to work wearing a jacket made out of an Axminster Carpet! An amazing thing that. When he took it off, he stood it up in the corner. It was so stiff. The world needed more Alans at that time.

I managed to con my way into helping the editors

175

whenever they'd let me and I was doing it just to get the experience really. I worked on film inserts on shows like *On The Buses, Catweazle, Please Sir?, Dick Turpin.* RICHARD O'SULLIVAN came in to watch us a couple of times. I liked him. He was so unassuming for a TV star.

I finally got a regular job as Assistant to the Presentation Editor, Phil Wilkinson. Our job was to cut feature films to allow commercial breaks to be inserted and sometimes we had to cut down the length of a film to fit a time slot. Once when Phil was on holiday, I was doing the editing and we had to cut-down that famous Western *The Horse Soldiers.* I had to take out about eight minutes. That's a lot of film.

Back to work on Monday after the film had been transmitted, switchboard came on the phone and said, I have a call for the Presentation Film Editor. That was me at the time. A very loud and forceful American voice came on the line saying, "Who the F**K do you think you are, cutting lumps out of my film?" Naturally, I asked to whom I was speaking and it came back, "This is JOHN FORD. I directed the damned thing!" Jeez, what do you say to JOHN FORD. One of the most famous and highly respected Film Directors ever. I was cacking myself. I explained that I was only doing the job that I was told to do and how sorry I was. Well he wanted names from above and heads were gonna roll. I managed to calm him down eventually and at the end of the week, I still had a job.

I had a memorable breakfast one Saturday morning when I was on stand-by. It was F.A. Cup Final day. I'm pretty sure Watford were in the final that day and I sat with BRIAN MOORE who was the ITV football commentator and a couple of the production team. Who should come and sit with us but ELTON JOHN! That's what makes me think that it was a Watford final because Elton was their Chairman at the time.

Elton John

Then JIMMY HILL, chief pundit of the ITV team came and sat down and then right out of the blue, who should arrive but FREDDIE STARR! Freddie was on the verge of stardom on the strength of his appearances one that very funny show *Who Do You Do?* A show made up of only impressionists. He had made records with Joe Meek like I did earlier in our careers but we didn't get round to talking about it. Freddie used to sing in front of a band called, FREDDIE STARR & THE MIDNIGHTERS.

It was possible, in those days, for me to watch inserts being recorded and later that day, Brian Moore was on the empty pitch at Wembley doing a link to camera, about the forthcoming match, when Freddie Starr walked across the pitch behind him dressed as Adolf Hitler but with shorts and wellies on! Brian was oblivious to this and then Freddie walked across again, but closer this time. Stopping to do a "Heil Hitler" salute. Then, he walked up to Brian, while he was talking, looked at the camera and proceeded to kiss Brian full on the lips! Quite one of the funniest things I had ever seen on live TV. He did a similar thing on another occasion when DICKIE DAVIS was doing a link to camera. *World Of Sport*, the ITV Saturday afternoon show had it's own permanent studio with a set where young

Freddie Starr (What a funny nutcase!)

girls sat behind typewriters supposedly typing information to be used by Dickie.

Freddie walked on behind Dickie, while he was talking, and began to talk to one of the girls in the second row. It got a bit amorous and they slipped down behind the desk. Next thing, Freddie was in view taking off his shirt. Then the typist did the same with her blouse! Then Freddie threw his trousers up in the air! Then her skirt followed suit! Freddie half stood up looking dishevelled, the girl dragged him down again and dear old Dickie soldiered on not realising what had been going on behind him!

There used to be a golfing joke "bandied around "the studios about Dickie Davis' golfing skills. It went like this, What goes put-put-put-put-put-put-put-put? Naturally, you'd think it was a Lambretta or a Vespa scooter. No. It was Dickie Davis playing golf! Cruel or what?

Freddie was a wonderfully funny, man but it got to the point where you just didn't know what he was going to do next. Unpredictable is the word I'm after.

SIMON DEE was at the very top of his tree at this time and was given his own show by LWT. He had a great house band fronted by MAYNARD FERGUSON, the world-renowned trumpeter. It was just like any other chat show really but he had a couple of "Dolly Birds" who used to

Simon Dee, a fallen Idol

walk the guests on to the set. I was there for the auditions for the girls and boy, were there some beauties! The trouble was that some only had two brain cells. The one who stuck out (bad choice of phrase!) was VALERIE LEON, later to become a Bond Girl and star of those famous commercials for Hai Karate after-shave. She was gorgeous but she didn't get a job on the *Simon Dee Show*. Shame.

A pair (bad choice of phrase again) known as The Baker Twins got the job. They weren't bad either!

Sometimes they needed a bit of film to play into the show and that was my job.

Simon had the famous German motor racing driver JOCHAN RINDT on the show because he had survived a monster crash with his car at The Indi 500 in the USA. We got the film and the director wanted to see it. So they bought it to our edit suite and put it on my Steinbeck machine. I sat with Jochan on one side, Simon stood behind and the director sat on the other.

Now the director was called Brian Izzard and he was outrageously camp. Surprise surprise! He used to wear bright yellow Rupert Bear trousers and a bright yellow

Rupert Bear scarf around his neck over a very RED jumper! He couldn't keep his hand off my knee while we were viewing the film. I had to keep moving it off and finally, I stopped the machine and said, "Brian, if you don't keep your hands to yourself, I'm gonna have to hit you!" "Sorry Love" he said," I was getting too excited and carried away." I could see that! And feel it!

One morning, I met up with an old friend from my days at The Star Club in Hamburg. The canteen was situated right in the middle of the studio complex. By that I mean that all the studios were at one end and all the technical areas and editing suites were at the other. So you went into the canteen from either end.

On this particular morning, I went in from my end and the door opened at the other, from the studio. There stood TONY ASHTON, the keyboard player from THE REMO 4. He was their doing a recording with his new band, ASHTON, GARDENER & DYKE. Their record in the charts was "Resurrection Shuffle". Tony saw me exactly as I saw him.

"F****IN' HELL!" He yelled out and we ran into a "man-hug" in front of everybody who stood open-mouthed at the scene. It was great to see him again and I was genuinely happy that his band was getting some success at last. We didn't have much time to chat but it was nice all the same.

We used to pick out small bits from the feature films to make promotion trailers and the promo directors took them to the department know as Presentation to have them topped & tailed and a voice-over added and finished off with some music behind. I liked doing this and I always had ideas to offer.

One day when I had just come back to work after a holiday, I was told that I had an interview that very afternoon for a job in Presentation/Transmission as an Assistant Transmission Controller! They had applied on my behalf while I was away. I wasn't actually dressed to interview for a job. 70s clothes weren't the most attractive. I had an orange shirt, ginger cord jeans, a chocolate coloured PVC jacket and a cravat of some kind! Nice!

One of the interviewers was a Transmission Controller named Alec Gunn. His claim to fame was that he had appeared in the wonderful Ealing Comedy, *The Lavender Hill Mob*. Alec was on screen for about one and a half minutes, driving a police car in the getaway scene. He drove just the same in real life actually. After a party, he and his wife Bay (White, who appeared in *Coronation Street*) said their goodbyes, went to their car, she got in the driving seat, switched on the hazard lights, then the indicators, then she released the bonnet catch. Then they both got out and changed places and Alec reversed away down the street! It's a damned good job there was no breathalyser test and very little traffic in those days. He was a lovely man who everybody liked and admired. He used to direct the transmission with all the flair and panache of a stage actor. Great fun to work with.

Anyway, I got the job. They were concerned about my "Nocturnal Activities", that is playing with a band but they liked me. I was well chuffed. It was a major increase in salary but it meant that I had to quit my other job with The George Bradley Band. They were about to start a first booking on The *Q.E.2.* That could have been quite an experience. But, once again music had to take a back seat in my life.

I had another interest too. We had another little baby girl called Karen born December 8th 1969.

Malcolm Lenny

Chapter 16   T.V. Transmission

The Presentation department was responsible for the actual transmission of all the material that went from the studios, to the transmitters and then to your homes. Material means, live studio shows, live sports events, basically any live outside broadcasts. Then there were the programmes recorded on two inch video tape, yes two inch! Feature films, transmitted from telecine projectors, 35mm & 16mm. Finally commercials transmitted from film mostly, with a few on tape. The commercials paid the wages, the rent and gave LWT an income to make more programmes.

After training for about six weeks on a vision and sound desk, I suddenly became aware that there were plans afoot to move the whole company to The South Bank TV Centre that was under construction already. This was a totally custom-built, self-contained complex that could handle everything LWT needed, under one roof. A wonderful undertaking. That place was a joy to work in and to have a job that I enjoyed so much as well was unbelievable.

London Weekend TV Studios. South Bank 1972

When the move did happen, LWT offered to pay moving expenses for any member of staff, who wanted to move South of the River Thames. I thought, Here's an opportunity and with somewhere like maybe Bromley, Kent in mind, we started looking.

Bromley was far too expensive for me so we ended up in Maidstone. "The county town" of Kent. That's what it said on the hand-bill I was given. It was much further out of London than I wanted to be but it was all I could afford at the time. Jane was five and Karen two and a half when we moved into a two bedroom, first floor maisonette. Not exactly luxurious but it did the job for the time being.

Jane was at infant's school and Karen was at playgroup when I got the call to play music again.

I auditioned for a job in a band, backing yet another of those "pretty boys". This one was called Johnny Apollo & The Premiers. The audition was held at The Astor Club in the West End of London. Mr Bertie Green, owner of the club, was backing the singer financially, so I thought it just might work. Bertie Green was one scary character. He seemed a bit like a London gangster. He controlled an awful lot of artistes including the wonderful Matt Monroe for a while. I was very nervous when I arrived, I opened my guitar case and revealed my trusty old Gibson 335 again, I got the job! I hadn't even played a note. Just having an instrument like that meant I had to be good. That band lasted about two gigs before I decided I couldn't carry on playing with a singer who had looks and absolutely nothing else but looks. It was like the Mike Sarne thing all over again.

The band all left together and re-formed once we got outside! Dickie Excell, on Tenor Sax, "Twiggy" Branch on Bass, Barry "the nutter" Jones, on Drums and me on Guitar. We did a few local gigs but it wasn't going to shake the planet so we split up after a few weeks.

There was a music shop in Maidstone called ESE that had a notice board for bands to find musicians or musicians to find bands. I took a card off the board for a band called HAPPY DAZE. What a great name for a band, I thought. I called them and they said to come along to the Chatham Dockyard Petty Officers Mess the following Saturday.

When I walked in I thought, This sounds a bit good. They had the usual line-up but they had a good lead vocalist and they had harmonies going on behind. It was very reminiscent of my days back in Germany with The Hi-Fi's. I told them I liked what I heard and they asked me to come to their next practice and do an audition.

Here we go again then. The practice was held in a garden shed about eight feet square. It was freezing! The drummer, Diz Izzard, sat in one corner with his Parka on and a woolly hat. I could hardly feel my strings and when we sang, you could see our breath like it was fog.

I sang a high, falsetto vocal backing to the Rita Coolidge song "I Don't Wanna Talk About It" and they asked me what else I could sing up high. I suggested The Four Seasons song "Sherry" and that was that. I was in the band. The other two were Len Turner (Lead Vocals) and Johnny (Putrid) Pritchard (Bass).

At this point of writing, that drummer and I have been together for more than 30 years! It's almost like being married to the same person for all that time but Dave "Diz" Izzard and me have weathered many storms together and we're still mates. We'd have to be because we can both be pedantic pains-in-the-butt at times.

Workwise, the job at LWT was really good. It was always

exciting because in effect we were "live" all the time and the buck stopped with us. We were in the unenviable position that if we made a mistake, we could screw up a multi-thousand pounds production! We were classified as the "nominated contractor" of the ITV network. Which meant most of the output of the network came through us before being re-routed out to the other regions.

Being in that area, I got to meet all kinds of personalities. Very early after starting a The South Bank Centre, I was walking across the underground car park when a voice said, "Excuse me dear, could you help me get to the 12th floor hospitality rooms?" It was the lovely old actress IRENE HANDEL.

She was just like my own favourite Auntie Laura from way back in my childhood. I offered her my arm and we walked to the lift together, chatting away. She was just like her on-screen personality. A lovely person and a little bit dizzy. She was starring in a children's comedy show called *Metal Mickey* all about a robot. It was directed by MICKEY DOLENZ from The Monkeys. That world-famous, manufactured pop group. I only got to meet Mickey fleetingly because he was too important to chat with us minions at that time.

Presentation used to also be responsible for making promotion trailers for forthcoming programmes, series and films etc.

One day, we were set to make some promos for a very prestigious programme which LWT had made of the Agatha Christie book *Why Didn't they ask Evans?*

The voice-over man was a guy called BILL MITCHELL. He had the voice that was used on the Carlsberg Lager commercials. You know, the very deep, gruff, American voice that said,

"Probably........., the best lager.......... in the world".

When Bill walked into our control room, he looked amazing! Over six feet tall, all dressed in black. Shirt, trousers, shoes, with a cape over his shoulders joined with a silver chain and in one hand a silver-topped waking stick, the other a glass of red wine.

Boy did he look the part or what? I was Sound Balancer that day and got just the right sound for Bill's voice. It was kind of chilling just to hear him say the title, "Why didn't they ask Evans?"

As I mentioned FREDDIE STARR before, I must tell you about an interview that he did, promoting the show *Who Do You Do?* One of our continuity announcers, PETER LEWIS, had to interview Freddie. Not the easiest thing to do. They sat opposite each other doing the question & answer bit quite straight and suddenly Freddie began to roll up his trouser leg. First one, then the other. Not content with that, he then leaned forward and started to do the same to Peter's trousers. Now Peter, being a consummate professional, soldiered on with the interview and there they both sat. Trousers neatly rolled up and four shiny white knees all on display. Freddie thought Peter wouldn't get through without corpsing, but he did. House point to Peter.

Our other continuity announcer was ALEC TAYLOR. Another, very experienced and trustworthy man under any circumstance. There was a comedy programme called *The Secret Life of Edgar Briggs* starring a fairly new, young actor named DAVID JASON. David was down to be interviewed by Alec live in our presentation studio.

I went with Alec to collect David at the lift. The doors

opened. David shouted, "That's the man!" Pointing at Alec. Leapt out and dragged Alec to the floor. He was already in character as the bungling person he portrayed in the show. We got him off and rushed him into the studio. The bungling carried on during the interview but the funniest point was when David took a fountain pen out of his pocket to pretend to write something. Of course the pen wouldn't work, he thumped it and shook it and then squirted it straight at Alec. Unfortunately, it went straight into Alec's mouth! He carried on, but for the next hour of live links to camera, he had BLUE TEETH!

That kind of thing would never happen today because TV Channels don't have in-vision announcers or any personality. Which is a great pity in my opinion.

Whenever new programmes were made and ready for transmission, the actors and actresses used to come in to our presentation studio, where the announcers used to sit, and do links or short interviews.

JANET STREET-PORTER was starting to make her appearance on a small London-based magazine programmes for LWT. One morning, she was doing the rounds and came into our Presentation Suite. "Where's

David Jason in The Top Secret Life of Edgar Briggs

Dickie Davis?" She said. "I want to add him to my list of Star F**ks." Ahem! What do you say to that? Nothing is the answer. Dickie was safe for the time being.

When *Dempsey & Makepeace* was scheduled for transmission, MICHAEL BRANDON and GLYNIS BARBER came in to do some promotions.

Michael was "Mr Cool" but Glynis was gorgeous! She looked great on the screen but up close and personal? WOW! She wore this low-cut dress in a silky sort of material. Again, I was sound operative so I had to clip a mike on her, somewhere. Well it had to go somewhere on the halter-neck strap but the cable, although very thin, was too obvious and had to be hidden. Alright, alright! Calm down! I didn't have the cheek to say that I needed to feed the cable either up or down her dress and she knew I was getting hot under the collar at the mere thought of it.

So she took the cable, with a cheeky, knowing smile and fed it under her dress while I averted my eyes. Honest I did! Phew. That was a tense moment that I'll never forget.

A couple of days later we had the equally lovely LORRAINE CHASE in the studio to do that same thing.

Gorgeous Glynis Barber from Dempsey & Makepiece

When I told her about the nearly embarrassing moment that I'd had with Glynis Barber, she just laughed and said, "You can stick yer 'and up my dress luv. Yer won't find nuffin there. It's like an ironing board".

Anuvver smashin' bird was Lorraine and a joy to work

The delightful Lorraine Chase, a very funny Lady

with. I'm very glad that she went on to do better things after her "Luton Airport" start to her career.

In the early days of London Weekend Television, DAVID FROST was not only a major shareholder but he had his own shows. *Frost on Friday, Frost on Saturday,* and oddly enough *Frost on Sunday.* All good shows in their own field.

On Saturday evening, after The ITN News, David would come up to our studio/control room to do a live trailer for his Sunday show. On one particular occasion, once again I was sound operative, David came to do his promo on the front of the commercial break and PETER JAY was doing a promo for *Weekend World*, the flagship current affairs Sunday morning show.

It was my job to play the theme music to both shows underneath the presenter while he was talking to camera. Well in those days there were no such things as MP3 players, iPODs etc. All I had was a quarter inch reel-to-reel tape recorder. So I had to pre-fade (that means make sure it finished right to the second), the music. So I marked up the *Weekend World* theme tune and put it on the shelf behind me and cued up the *Frost on Sunday* music.

Up comes David with his theme nicely underneath him. He, and it, finished perfectly together.

He vacates the chair. Peter Jay slips into place. Meanwhile, I'm into the commercials and watching the levels. I've got 2 minutes and ten seconds. At a convenient moment, I take the *Frost* music off the tape deck and put the *Weekend World* music on.

Now if you remember the music, it was a fairly hard piece of rock instrumental called "Nantucket Sleighride" by Mountain. Which ran up to a crescendo and a natural finish. Guess what? I put it on the wrong way round so it was backwards!

Peter Jay comes up in vision and there's this 'Orrible noise underneath his voice which, instead of coming to a proper end, kinda petered out into nothing.

I felt very silly and held my head in shame.

Mistakes like that were a rarity especially from me. I was good at the job!

"Nantucket Sleigh Ride" introduced me to another personality at LWT.

The Head of Music Services was a well-known and respected musical director, arranger and composer called HARRY RABINOWITZ. I remembered his name from post-war radio shows like *Workers Playtime*, when I was a kid and he had worked his way up throughout the years to a position of some importance. He always looked a bit eccentric in appearance, with a tidy beard and thinning hair combed forward into a fringe. His dress was also a fair bit arty.

The head of my department sent me to him to see if I could do a music-editing job for him. This was to take out all of the vocals from the song, leaving just the instrumental. We could use the music for making other *Weekend World* promos or we could use it in case there was a breakdown during the actual programme. No mean feat, but I managed it OK.

I told Harry about my past and present musical life and we became sort of friends. He used to call me "The Old Rock'n'Roller". I appreciated that even though I was only in my very early 30's.

The lovely Miss PAM RHODES became one of our continuity announcers. Now Pam is one of the nicest ladies you could ever wish to meet. Beautiful with that soft "lisp" in her voice that made you hang on her every word. I was so pleased when she got the job of presenting *Songs Of Praise* for the BBC later in her career.

One day, we had the brilliant ALAN BENNETT in to do a promotion for his soon-to-be-aired play *Doris & Doreen.* His North-country accent sounded funny enough but his script was hilarious!

After talking about the play, he ended by saying, "So if I'm not rinsing my vest or doing my foot, I'll be watching *Doris & Doreen*. Will you?" I became an instant fan of Mr Bennett and I've seen many of his plays and read his books too. A very talented man, in my humble opinion.

Chapter 17   Saturday Morning Television

In the early '70s there wasn't really any Saturday morning television for kids. The in-vision announcers would simply introduce the programmes. Then LWT had some sort of contract with Walt Disney to play short clips from their films in between programmes like *THUNDERBIRDS* or *STINGRAY* or *BLACK BEAUTY* etc.

We began to transmit Jim Henson's *SESAME STREET* which was an instant hit with the kids. Let's face it, it was a very funny show, with great characters like Kermit the Frog, Grover, Big Bird, Oscar the Grouch, Ernie & Bert etc, as well as being sort of educational. This was long before *THE MUPPETS SHOW.*

One of our Telecine Engineers, Ian Dobson, came back from holiday in the U.S.A., with a glove puppet of the COOKIE MONSTER from *Sesame Street*. He bought it into our control room to show us. I put my hand up inside it and did a fairly passable imitation of the voice that went with it. That was it! Wendy Powell, our Transmission Controller for the day, said, "Right Malcolm, get in the studio with Alec Taylor, the announcer, with COOKIE and do the link into *Sesame Street!*"

To hear is to obey. In I went, down on the floor beside the desk and held a conversation, as COOKIE, with Alec linking into the show. Everyone thought it was funny so I carried on throughout the morning, linking in and out of all the kid's programmes. We used Jacob's Cream Crackers as "cookies" simply because I could make more mess on the announcers desk with them.

Wendy covered the vision mixing, which should have been me on that day. She used to be a vision mixer in her early days in T.V. at Alexander Palace for the BBC.

What we didn't know was that outside out "gallery" window, the Controller of Programmes, Cyril Bennett, arrived with his two sons to show them what went on in live television. He came in and said, "Wendy, what are you doing?" She said, "We've got this puppet and Malcolm's doing the links with it. It's really good and funny too"

Cyril said, "Wendy, it probably is really good and funny

but you'll have to stop or Jim Henson will sue our backsides off! "We stopped. No one was sacked. We didn't get sued but LWT started to look seriously about doing a proper Saturday morning show for kids.

Very soon, *SATURDAY SCENE* was born. Presented by the delicious Miss SALLY JAMES. I say delicious because Sally was a great, fun, bird of delicious proportions! What she didn't realise was that when she wore her T-shirt with *SATURDAY SCENE* across the front, all that could been seen was *TURD*! Ahh, the innocence of it all.

My two Daughters, Jane and Karen when to see Walt Disney's *Robin Hood* at the Leicester Square Theatre with Sally James. They went as special guests with some competition winners. They loved it and met Robin (The Fox) and Little John (The Bear).

The Saturday mornings used to have known pop stars who were in the hit-parade at the time and up-and-coming stars of the future. One of the new bands was PILOT. Who had a couple of monster hits with "January" and "It's Magic". They were seriously talented guys.

Old friend, Alan Clarke, of The Hollies, came in and we

Lovely, madcap Sally James from LWT's Saturday Show

met once again. He was surprised to find me working in television.

Freddie Garrity, from Freddie & The Dreamers, came in to do an interview with Sally and we reminisced about that outdoor festival that we'd both been on back in the early 60s. My work-mates always thought it was amusing that I knew and was known by quite a lot of the artists who came in.

The biggest band of the mid-70s was THE BAY CITY ROLLERS. LWT organised a "special" ROLLERS DAY. The street outside the studios was like a football crowd! Maybe a 1,000 girls packed around the front doors. The noise was deafening! The Rollers came in through the scene dock and up to our control room. Oddly enough, they weren't exactly full of personality. I think they were in shock about their amount of success in such a short time.

They were only kids really, but we got some interviews done and they were gone.

One of the most popular shows running on ITV at the time was *The Partridge Family*. DAVID CASSIDY might have had something to do with it? He was getting hit records so he came to the UK and LWT signed him up to do *Saturday Scene*. When he arrived at the studios it was like "Rollers Day" all over again! But this time it was "David Cassidy Day" and all the same girls turned up to have another scream. When he was ushered into our little studio, he was flanked by two massive body- guards who weren't gonna let anyone get near young David. Well I had to! Because I had to get a lapel mike on him as I did with everyone else. They watched me like a hawk, just in case I cut off a lock of his hair and sold it to the fans outside. David was very relaxed and he was very helpful to me and we did some really nice links between the programmes.

One other "special day" was "GARY GLITTER DAY". Gary was getting big hits and an even bigger following from his fans who became known as his gang. "Rock'n'Roll Part 1", "I Love You, Love Me Love" and "D'you Wanna Be In My Gang?" I hadn't seen him since when we were back in Hamburg at The Star Club. When he came in, he was plonked down in his chair and I proceeded to point a floor mike up at him. I looked up at him and said, "Mornin' Raver!" (because his name was Paul Raven back in Hamburg). He looked at me, quizzically for a moment and then recognition came over his face. "F**k me", He said, "What are you doing here?" "Working", Says I. Once again, we had a chat about old times and I reminded him of the time when me and my old pal from The Hi-Fi's, Mel Wright, had picked him up off the floor of one of the bars after a couple of sherberts and almost carried him back to

The Pacific Hotel.

In those days Paul Gadd, aka Paul Raven, aka Gary Glitter was a real fun guy and I'm proud to say I new him and I liked him. What has happened in later years is beyond my comprehension. The least said the better.

SHOWADDYWADDY were another up-and-coming band, who were all fun guys. I hadn't met them before but it didn't stop me meeting them later when my band HAPPY DAZE supported them at a gig later on.

The head of my department, used to get more than a little bit upset that so many of his pop stars seemed to have known me in a previous existence. But that's just because I played in a couple of bands, with a little bit of success and frankly, I got around to a lot of places.

The marvellous KENNY EVERETT came in one morning and all I can say is that he was a genius! That word is banded about so much in the media but believe me, it certainly applied to Kenny. We talked about his radio shows because I used to love the way he multi-tracked his own voice and produced very creditable pop sounds that would have put several "stars" of the day, to shame. We got on so well that, at the end of the morning, Kenny gave me a quarter inch tape of some of his "Jingles". I'm proud to say that I still have it today. Long may his memory continue.

Saturday Scene grew in popularity week by week until it became hard work as well as enjoyment. The Transmission Staff, were responsible for the smooth running of all the links in and out of programmes and the commercial revenue was increasing. So, we thought we would ask for some kind of extra payment for our efforts. That was it! Money? No Way! The upshot of that was that it was taken out of our little Presentation studio and put into one of the main studios. Using a full studio crew and, no doubt, costing much more to produce than if they had left it where it was. Oh well, we had our moment and we had a lovely time doing it.

I mentioned BARRY HAYNES a bit earlier. He became one of our regular continuity announcers. He was first known for doing his "bit" on the original *Come Dancing*. It was Barry's job to sit up in "the Gods", in his Dinner suit and talk about each of the contestants. That is, who they were, where they came from and who had sewn on every sequin by hand.

There's a lovely story about Barry and the very early days of *THE TUBE* on Channel 4 . Jools Holland & Paula Yates used to introduce it. It was late in the evening and we all know that Jools got told off for using a 4-letter word.

Anyway, this particular show finished with a band that was severely lacking in talent but not in volume! Barry came up in vision straight after it and with genuine cynicism, said, Well, WASN'T….. THAT….. GOOD! meaning it was really shite. The next day, there was a memo for Barry from upstairs, which told him, Not to make <u>Facticious</u> remarks! Well he had done just that. It was a fact that the band was crap. What the secretary was meant to write was <u>facetious</u> remarks.

We all had a good laugh about that. My Dad used to say, "The thousands I spend on your education and you speak like that!" I only went to a "common-or-garden" state Infants/Primary school which didn't open until I was six, due to Mr Hitler and his plans for world domination. My Secondary school wasn't much better but I did alright. I always maintain that I didn't really start to develop as a person until I got out in the world and started to work for a living. Plus being involved in music was a big thing for me.

Back to Barry Haynes and one of Barry's own favourite true stories was about an Irish bus driver who auditioned for an announcer's job. It goes like this, the guy had to read from autocue.................He fluffed his words and said, "Oh Balls!"
"Oh Shit, I've said Ball"s
"Oh F**k, I've said Shit. Who wants to be an announcer anyway!" and walked out!

Priceless!

Barry had an extraordinary incident one New Years Eve. He decided to wear his full dinner suit for his link at midnight and open a bottle of champagne to toast the viewers for A Happy New Year. Now, drinking was frowned upon by the powers that be, up in the tower block where they all sat behind their desks, making momentous decisions. We had a remote controlled camera, with a pan & tilt head, that was controlled by the Transmission controller in the control room.

Barry comes up in vision, in all his glory, dressed up to the nines. Proceeds to strip off the foil and the wire holding in the cork. Of course, BANG! It goes all over Barry, all over the desk and worst of all, all over the camera! It still worked but Barry looked like he was under water. Needless to say, we never wished the viewer A Happy New Year again with anything stronger that coffee after that.

Chapter 18   Experts And Pundits etc.

Before football became the industry that it is today, 2017, LWT used to transmit a programme called *The Big Match*, presented by Brian Moore.

I know that the BBC had *Match of the Day* (and still does) but I like to think that we had the first and best bunch of experts, pundits, know-alls or whatever you want to call them.

Jimmy "The Chin" Hill was Chairman, Derek Dougan, Paddy Crerand and Malcolm Allison made up the panel. There were occasional changes periodically, like when one of the regulars was not available, they would bring in Liam Brady and later, as a permanent addition, dear old Brian Clough. Cloughie was a brilliant raconteur and the others used to wind him up something awful! We all know that he used to like a glass of something once in a while but it never interfered with his expert analysis of a game or his opinion of a player.

Brian Moore Ace Football Commentator and nice guy!

The on-air exchanges between the guys were always fun to watch but sometimes they would run out of time and continue when they got to the bar after the show. I was with them one evening and I had got to the bar just before them. The doors to the bar were shoved open and the voices were at fever pitch! Yelling at each other at the top of their voices. Obviously there was a slight disagreement going on. To anyone who didn't know them, you'd think that a fight was going to happen any minute! Cloughie and Dougan were the main participants and Big Mal Allison was egging them on. Paddy Crerand could see what was happening and he was laughing behind his hand. I really thought that they were coming to blows so I said, "Right, who wants a drink then?" And it all petered out in a second. I'm still not sure that it wasn't a set-up to get me to buy everyone a drink but it worked.

Dear old Brian Moore used to get some stick from the guys all because he was a Gillingham FC supporter! Now that just wasn't fair. Somebody had to support Gillingham and he was it.

One evening, I was switching in the slow-motion video disc into the Mid-Week Match, and we had a visit from the West Ham Utd. Manager RON GREENWOOD and his assistant JOHN LYALL, who later became Manager himself.

Mr Greenwood had my absolute respect because he had let one of my old school friends "try out" for West Ham. Ron was an absolute gentleman who knew the game of football inside-out. While we were waiting for the match to kick off, we were all talking about tactics.

Ron asked everyone, "Where is the space on a football field?" We were all saying things like, "At the corner flags" "Behind the full backs" etc. His answer was, "Between two players!" How simple is that? Absolutely true of course.

In those days, I used to love football with a passion. That love has been killed off because it has become just an industry. Teams frequently only have two or three home bred players and the rest are "Ifskis, Ofskis, Ellies or Bellies, Umberto or Umbongo". Club football has become the be-all and end-all of the game. The National team doesn't seem to matter any more. D'you know, I'm really glad that I saw England win The World Cup in 1966 because I don't think it'll ever happen again simply because young home-bred footballers just don't get the chance to get into a premier or league team. Clubs keep buying in ready-made foreign players who can win games for the club and it doesn't matter about the National team.

As I write this chapter, England, have failed to qualify to play in the 2008 European Cup! There are TV ads asking, "Who are you gonna support?" That's disgraceful!

I had better shut up about football because I'll only offend someone.

Around this time, I was asked to do a bit of "moonlighting" for the BFBS. That's the British Forces Broadcasting Service to you. It used to happen at the LWT outside broadcast studio at Wickham Road, Wembley. Everything was recorded on tape and sent by courier out to Germany to be transmitted locally.

One particular morning, I was due to be Directing an interview with that fine actor, PETER EGAN. He was already well known for his part in *Ever Decreasing Circles* as the cool and sexy next-door neighbour to the hapless Richard Briers. He was in to be interviewed about his current role as *Prince Regent*, in the TV series. Nine thirty in the morning, in he walks. Smack on time to the second, looking so cool and sexy that I could hear the two girls who were working with me, melting where they stood! No one has the right to have that kind of effect on women! Only Sean Connery and Pierce Brosnan or George Clooney

Peter Egan (The Ladies man)

maybe. Ask my wife Maureen, but I'm unlikely to meet them in my lifetime. Anyway, we talked about the interview and the girls began to relax I think that was probably due to the bottle of "screw-top Soave" that had appeared from out of the office fridge. The interview was perfect and wrapped up in no time at all. When Peter had to leave, I almost had to drag the girls off him to let him go! Not a dry eye in the house. Some years later, I saw Peter in a production of the wonderful play *ART* and he was just as funny, cool and sexy……….. Oh shut up!

In 1972, after I had changed jobs and moved to Maidstone, I worked quite a lot with the band that I joined and still play with now, HAPPY DAZE. How the hell I managed to sometimes do a gig on the Saturday night and then a full day shift at LWT without falling asleep is a mystery to me but I did it very often. I loved my music every bit as much as I loved my job.

We used to play on the same bills as quite a lot of known bands and artists like JOE BROWN, who we did a new Years Eve dance at a glass manufacturers in Snodland. Not exactly the Palladium I know but it was a good gig. Joe was exactly as the world knows him. A cheeky chappie, a great guitarist and another consummate professional. Even after we were all told that we had to change in the kitchen together. No dressing room for the star or the support band. That's the way it goes.

We did a show at The Savoy Hotel in The Strand, for Great Ormond Street Hospital for children. Now that was a classy joint. All gilt paint and velvet covered chairs.

We played for dancing and the cabaret was that Irish nut-case FRANK CARSON! I say nut-case because Frank never knows when to stop. He was hilarious and they had to drag him off after half an hour or he would still be there now!

I fist met Frank Carson in1987 when I went to N.Ireland to play golf with LWT against all the other ITV companies at Royal County Down.

Frank was a guest speaker for the evening but he did play too. I didn't actually play with him but my good mate Pat Brennan did and he said golf was impossible! Frank didn't let up for a minute. Joke after joke after joke! I met up with him in the bar later in the evening and there were about eight of us doing a "last man standing" kind of thing. My face really hurt from laughing and I used up all the good jokes that I new on Frank but he just kept going. We had to call in a night at about two thirty in the morning. We had to be back on the tee at eight thirty! Frank left us after the second day, thank goodness, and he gave Pat a leaving present. It was a head cover for a 13 .5 wood! Now, anyone who knows about golf knows there's no such club! That's the kind of man Frank Carson was.

Another guest speaker was that great Rugby Union player WILLIE JOHN McBRIDE. To have my hand crushed in a hand-shake and to stand in the shadow of such a big man in size and in stature was enough for me!

HAPPY DAZE also played at a function in Hitchin, Herts, where MIKE READ was the cabaret. Our bass player, Melvin Hann, was a great fan of Mike's and simply had to have his photo taken with the man. Mike did about 40 minutes and surprisingly, he wasn't "blue". A lot of comedians rely upon filth to get them through. OK he was a bit risque but inoffensive. I liked him as much as I did on *The Comedians* TV show. That was quite a few years before he got his acting career going on *East Enders*.

We did a couple of "special shows" down at Hastings on

the pier where there was a massive old fashioned ballroom. I remember playing it with THE PACKABEATS back in the 60s. The Dave Clark Five had their two monster hits with "Glad All Over" and "Bits And Pieces" at the time. Of course we had to play Glad as part of our set. Believe me the stomping of the crowd had to be experienced, to be believed!

It was so heavy that the Manager of the pier told us to, "Stop! Or you'll have us all in the sea!" I have to admit it was a bit scary. So we stopped.

When we did it with HAPPY DAZE, we were the local support band to THE FOUNDATIONS and BRIAN POOLE and The Electrics. I think we did three spots. One before The Foundations, one in the middle before Brian Poole and one at the end before handing over to my good mate Stan Lee King, the best Disc Jockey in Kent!

Do you remember me telling you how THE PACKABEATS played Brian Poole's hit, "Do You Love Me" just before he came on at Southall? Well we did it again with HAPPY DAZE. The crowd were yelling for us because we had worked them so well with one song after another with hardly a second in between. Brian said, "I'm not going on after that. Get the DJ to do 15 minutes!"

He was alright in the end and we hadn't done it deliberately to upset him but I must say we did play up a storm.

We played there again later on that summer, supporting THE FORTUNES and EDISON LIGHTHOUSE. Once again, if you remember, THE PACKABEATS played with The Fortunes on our first Scottish tour back in '62. They were good then and they still were 25 years later. I always loved their harmonies and there were four original members too. We had a reminisce about the old times and they kindly said that they remembered The Packabeats back then.

EDISON LIGHTHOUSE of course were not the original group who made "Love Grows Where My Rosemary Goes". That was made by session men including CLEM CATTINI, drummer from The Tornados and the lead voice was TONY BURROWS who sang with The Pipkins ("Gimme Dat Ding") White Plains ("My Baby Loves Love") "United We Stand" (Brotherhood of Man) Etc. It didn't matter because the band EDISON LIGHTHOUSE, gave an excellent performance and they were a credit to the name.

I met up with CLIFF BENNETT again when we did a gig at The Lees Cliffe Hall, Folkestone. I hadn't seen Cliff since my very early days playing at Kew Boathouse in the late 50s. I tell a lie! I did play on the same bill at Putney "Brawlroom" and at Southall Community Centre in the early '60s. How soon I forget.

Cliff had a barrel chest and he fairly ROARED his way through his set. Naturally we talked about the old days and what fun we had. By then, it had become just a job to Cliff. MARMALADE were on the bill at Folkestone too and what a good band they were. For a start, they looked professional. All suited & booted as we say and once again their harmony singing was excellent. I mentioned that one of the singers with The George Bradley Band, back in '70/'72, RUBY JAMES, had sung with Junior Campbell who used to lead Marmalade. They seemed to recollect her, which was nice.

I also did a spin-off duo with Len Turner who was vocalist/rhythm guitarist with HAPPY DAZE. That was called Sounds Familiar. Well it did! We did a little club called The Pink Elephant somewhere near Tenterden in Kent, which was owned by PETER HOWARTH. He was

225

the good-looking son Joey in the TV show *Bread*. He made us feel very much at home in his club. He even sang a couple of songs with us. Many years later, Peter took the place of the great ALAN CLARKE when he retired from The HOLLIES.

Around this time, I had a terrible family happening followed by a lovely one. My eldest daughter Jane had a burst appendix and peritonitis. She almost died! But for the fact that she was such a strong little nine year old, she might not have made it. At the same time, in the same hospital, my wife was giving birth to our third daughter Sue. So I had one upstairs trying not to die and another downstairs trying to be born. That was a very testing time.

Chapter 19   More Faces At LWT

Although I enjoyed my job as an Assistant Transmission Controller, I began to think I could do with a bit more cash so I asked for an attachment to the sound department. I'd always had a hankering to be in production and I thought sound might be the way to go. I was allowed a six-week period, which was very generous from my head of Presentation and likewise from the head of Sound.

My first bit of action was on that funny show *Game For A Laugh*. I was allowed to sit in the gallery and watch The Sound Supervisor, Paul Faraday, at work. It was magic stuff. Live bits in front of the studio audience, film and video inserts played in. This was a new world to me. I was allocated to the guys who controlled the mikes that were set up above the audience. During the final recording of the show, they would single out the seat where the loudest laughter was coming from and "boost" it so it sounded even funnier. I got introduced to SARAH KENNEDY,

MATHEW KELLY and HENRY KELLY, but JEREMY
BEADLE was always just that little bit too busy to meet
every Tom, Dick & Harry who came his way. Nevertheless
he was very good at his job and the ratings proved that
point.

My next bit of action was an O.B. that's an Outside
Broadcast to the uninitiated. I was outside with the crew
who, were recording a bit of film for *The Gentle Touch*, the
police series of the moment.

The star, JILL GASCOINE, always looked lovely on-screen
but up close and personal, she was gorgeous! Those eyes! I
had to run down the road and into a pub somewhere in the
East End with a NAGRA tape recorder hanging on a strap
round my neck, trying to keep up with the guy who held
the "Fish Pole" mike. Let me tell you that NAGRA weighed
a bloody Ton! But Gill's eyes made it all worthwhile.

After *The Gentle Touch*, I was moved on to be part of the
most prestigious dram serial that LWT had undertaken for
a long while. It was called *The Winds Of War*. Known by all
members of staff as *The War in Windsor*. I was given the
none-too-easy job of controlling the boom mike for an
indoor studio scene. You don't realise what skill is

involved in what seems like a simple task, until you do it yourself.

Jill Gascoine in The Gentle Touch

I had seen so many "takes" halted with the cry from the Lighting Director, in a totally bored tone of voice, "Shadows Sound!" Which meant that the poor sound operator had managed to get a shadow of his mike or boom on the scenery. With the amount of lighting around the set it wasn't easy, believe me. My scene took place in a corridor with an actor and an actress. When they appeared for the take, it was the very beautiful VICTORIA

TENNANT and that mighty Hollywood legend ROBERT MITCHUM!

Boy. Was I scared or what! They did their bit in about five minutes flat and they were gone. I must have done alright because no one said anything.

I did get to meet the great Mr Mitchum a few weeks later when I had reason to burst into the office of the Assistant Head of Presentation, Vincent O'Brien with a query regarding transmission. Vincent had someone sitting with his back to the door and I burst in with a, "Sorry Vince but..........." He said, "I'd like you to meet Malcolm Lenny, one of our Transmission Controllers".

The man stood up, and up and up! He was massive! The size of a wardrobe! He turned and it was ROBERT MITCHUM. He offered me his hand, which was the size of a builder's shovel and just said,"Hi", in a deep, gruff American voice.

I was speechless and when I retrieved my crushed fingers from his vice-like grip, I offered my apologies and backed out of the office, like I was leaving an audience with royalty.

Robert Mitchum, the Mountain of a Man

Back to my stint with the Sound boys. Next, it was the most exciting thing musically that I had ever heard. I was put with a Sound Supervisor named Vick Finch and I went with him to a sound stage somewhere in the West End to see the recording of the Title and background music for *The Stanley Baxter Show*. Stanley was right at the peak of his television career at that time and had massive viewing figures. Vick had something like a 24 channel desk with another 24 channels on a sub-mixer. The orchestra seemed enormous. About 36 people I think. Boy it was magical to hear.

Afterwards, I was invited to have dinner at The Spaghetti House in Goodge Street with STANLEY BAXTER, the Director JOHN KAYE COOPER , the Musical Director ALYN AINSWORTH (known as "The Silver Fox" because of his magnificent Silver hair) Vick Finch, the Sound Supervisor and little me, Mr Nobody. It was one of the funniest, alcoholic, gastronomic and long dinners I've ever had. Just brilliant!

I had joined the LWT Golf Society and occasionally we would have guest players join us. NIGEL LITHGOE (The original Mr Nasty from talent shows) was a staff Light Entertainment Director, who came out to play once in a while and on one occasion, he brought the one and only JESS CONRAD with him as his guest. Jess did his usual entrance with a, "Hello Fans!" We all laughed of course because Jess was like that and he was harmless. I was put on the same table for dinner and we rambled on about our time together on The Hollies tour back in '64 when I was in The Hi-Fi's.

I'm sure we bored the pants off everyone else but we didn't care.

Two famous men worked on the musical side for LWT. One was MAX HARRIS who wrote loads of theme tunes for LWT shows and the other was LAURIE HOLLOWAY who, among other things, became Michael Parkinson's musical Director and he was married to the delightful Marian Montgomery. I was able to have a lovely round of golf one society day with both gentlemen. I use the word gentlemen very easily, because that's exactly what they were.

Many years later, LWT Golf Society went to the Golf Show at the NEC in Birmingham and afterwards we had a round of golf at a local club where the guest players were MALCOLM GREGSON and RONAN RAFFERTY. They didn't actually play the round but Malcolm was on a tee where you bet yourself against him with your longest drive and Ronan was on a par three where you bet yourself against him to go nearest the pin. I nearly had Ronan! It was a matter of two inches that he beat me by. But I got nowhere near Mr Gregson's drive. Not even when we teed off the yellow tee and he off the competition tee, 35yds further back! Nevertheless they were nice guys and it was a pleasure to meet them.

We used to record, what were called "Christmas Messages" in our presentation suite. This meant that artistes who were making shows in summer/autumn at LWT for transmission in December, would be asked to record a "Happy Christmas to all our viewers". We had DICKIE DAVIES, from *World Of Sport*, BRUCE FORSYTH from whatever game show he was doing at the time, I must say that Bruce was an absolute joy to work with and couldn't do enough to please everyone.

PAUL NICHOLAS, who was in such a hurry to be somewhere else that he got up to walk away without taking his lapel mike off and nearly strangled himself!

LENNY BENNETT and GERRY STEPHENS, who were a double act before Lenny went on to do *Punchlines* on his own, were very funny. I remember Lenny singing a version of "Rudolph The Brown-nosed Reindeer", which was untransmittable!

HUGHIE GREEN came in with a few pretty girls in attendance, plus the little girl who used to work with him on his shows called MONICA ROSE. Mr Green was not the nicest of people and he was downright rude to poor Monica. He constantly kept on reminding her that she was nothing without him etc. while all the time he was pawing the other girls about. Not one of my favourites.

CILLA BLACK was making the switch from being just a singer to an all round entertainer. She was very personable in those days. She came into our Presentation control room to make promos for her shows. Her "Scouse" accent grated on the ears a fair bit. It was exaggerated I'm sure. I had worked with many Liverpudlians throughout my years in music and I don't remember any talking quite like "our Cilla". Not everybody's cup of tea but don't take anything away from Cilla. What she did, she did very well and don't forget that *SURPRISE! SURPRISE!* Topped the TV ratings.

Working at a top class TV company like LWT, often meant that I would literally bump into all sorts of well known people. When the RUSSELL HARTY SHOW was a ratings topper, he often had great stars as his guests. Sometimes the not-so-great stars would also appear. I remember one night, I was walking down the corridor on my way to the control room behind a man who's shoulders almost touched both walls! He turned to come back the same way and it was the boxer, BILLY WALKER. He was a really nice cockney bloke who would spare a bit of his time with anyone.

"The Fonz" on The Russell Harty Show

Later the same evening, I was coming back from the bar with a tray of beers for the gang on transmission (after News at 10!) and who should appear and hold the door for me than THE FONZ, HENRY WINKLER.

Such a little guy compared to his character in *Happy Days*. As I went through the door, I said, "Thanks very much Mister Fozerelli," and all he said was, "Heeeeeeeeey" in true FONZIE style. It was my own special moment.

I kinda "bumped into" that great Englishman HENRY COOPER when he was appearing on Russell's show. All that's been said about 'Enery, is absolutely true. He was ordinary Henry then, but I met him again, twice, many years later when he was Sir Henry Cooper and he was just the same bloke.

The first time, I was going into my local Post Office and I held the door for him to come through. He had just been buying his National Lottery tickets! He obviously needed the dosh!

Another massive pair of shoulders that I stood next to in a lift belonged to ARNOLD SCHWARTZENEGGAR. There was barely any room for anyone else! He was due to appear on *The Russel Harty Show* on the strength of his movie *Pumping Iron*. Who could have imagined that he would be the Govenor of California, one day?

One of my very favourite 'Lift' stories goes like this. I was travelling from the ground floor up to our office on the 12th. Bit by bit, it was getting more full. One of the LWT Designers, Tony Crutchly, was at the back of the lift. It stopped, and in got one of our cleaners. A really big, black guy, in his white dust coat and pink Marigold gloves, carrying a yellow bucket and a mop. The bucket smelled very strongly of disinfectant. From the back of the lift, Tony Crutchly was heard to say, in a very "camp" voice, "I just love the smell of Brut, first thing in the morning, don't you? "The whole lift just collapsed! You couldn't write this stuff. It just happens.

One Christmas Eve, one of our Heads of Light Entertainment, David Bell, dropped into our control room to wish us Merry Christmas and bring us a bottle of champagne. He came in, looked around at the announcers backing "flat" whereupon somebody had nailed two holly wreaths because he had forgotten to buy a Christmas tree. David said, "Merry Christmas everyone..........What the F**K is that!" Because David had such a lovely soft Edinburgh accent, once again, we were all on the floor killing ourselves laughing.

I was actually on Transmission on the night that the wonderful TOMMY COOPER died at the ITV show *Live From Her Majesty's*. Everyone knows what happened back then but it's not common knowledge that as Tommy collapsed, we in Transmission had to take a commercial break to relieve the situation. Donny Osmond was due to follow Tommy but didn't feel able to go straight on. So always the consummate professional with the "show must go on" attitude, JIMMY TARBUCK went out and did five minutes of fill. Wonderful!

Oh, Dear Reader, Television was so different and frequently such fun in those days before it became a licence to print money. But that's another story.

Chapter 20   Goodbye To London Weekend Television

As Television "progressed", it got more and more impersonal from the point of view of the viewer. Our crew of Vision Mixer, Sound Balancer and Transmission Controller, Presentation Secretary and in-vision Announcer, was slowly whittled down to three people, then two then one. Computers had arrived and what used to be a slick, well executed transmission, turned into a "Wham Bam" sort of affair with abrupt cuts and no attention paid to sound balancing at all. That's when the viewer started to sit with his remote control in his hand cutting the levels of commercials and promos every time they appeared. We used to call it "Knife & Fork editing". It was a crying shame that Television had come to that but I suppose it's a bit like the Industrial Revolution when workers were very anti any change to their working methods.

Staff was being cut down everywhere, in all departments

and me? I was made redundant. That really upset me. I wasn't wanted any more by the company that I kind of "loved" in a way. We all used to work for, as well as with, each other. I simply couldn't work ten hour shifts including overnights, because I had a young family and it seemed to me that I wouldn't be able to see so much of them. That meant an awful lot to me, so I went.

Rupert Murdoch had just begun his satellite channel Sky. So I got a job there. Not in transmission but in the department that edited programmes to fit time slots and made promotions for the four channels that he started with. They were SKY ONE, EUROSPORT, SKY NEWS & THE MOVIE CHANNEL. It was firstly based at a company called TVI in Wardour Street, Soho, London. It was great fun, once again helping to get a TV company started like I had at LWT.

I met a crazy videotape editor there once. His name was Mikola Powluk, sorry man, if that's not how you spell it. He and I had to edit the USA Superbowl into a transmittable size programme for the UK. The actual event takes about four or five hours to complete, by the time they've had all the rigmaroll before, after and during the game itself. We sat in the edit suite, watching and logging every second of the event, bored ridgid! We ate two Chinese meals we were there so long. It was awful but we got it done.

After a short while in Wardour Street, SKY moved out to a custom-built complex at Isleworth, West of London. Sky was transmitting SKY Channel (Later SKY 1), SKY News, The Movie Channel and Eurosport. As a company, it wasn't doing very well. People didn't want to put a dish on their chimney. It looked ugly and viewers were reluctant to change from their usual BBC 1 & 2, ITV & Channel 4. We British are funny like that.

One Sunday morning, I was sitting in the coffee lounge with a few of the editing staff, when who should walk in but Mr Rupert Murdoch himself! White open-necked shirt and sleeves rolled up three-quarter style. "Listen up everybody" he said. This SKY TV is about as important to me as a branch of Sainsburys on the Outer Hebrides would be to them. So make it work or I'll shut it down!"

Make it work? Us? How could we make it work? The programming was fairly cr**ppy but that wasn't down to us!

He had a competitor in the shape of British Satellite Broadcasting. BSB as it was known. You know, the one with The 'Squariel'. How soon we forget. Well he bought it out in what was called a merger. We, the SKY staff, were all told that our jobs were safe. Wrong! What was known as a merger, became a MURDER! The axe fell and if you were the wrong side, you were gone. No consideration for experience or anything. Goodbye! I was the wrong side so I went.

Murdoch's money won him the day in the end when he bought football away from BBC & ITV simply because he had so much money and the others couldn't/wouldn't compete with him. Once he had the football "fraternity" with dishes, his way was open to do what he liked and television as I knew it was finished forever. I could go on about the dumbing down of television programming but that would only make you think that I'm a Grumpy Old Man and I'm not. One has to accept that things do change and nothing stays the same forever.

So began the two years of my life that I would like to forget. Redundant for the second time, right before Christmas too. Shortly after Christmas, my dear old Mum died aged 86. Then one of my two dogs, Buster, died. My daughter Karen's fiancee died in her arms aged 22! To cap it all, my first wife left me for a 28 year old Czechoslovakian folk dancer who worked in a sandwich bar! two days after our 25th wedding anniversary where we had a party of about 80 family and friends.

After about six months, he hopped off back to Prague. Usual stuff, female mid-life crisis. There was no way I'd have her back after what she'd done to me. When I think about it now (which isn't very often) it sounds just like a comedy script.

I had to go and "sign on" at the local Job Centre to get help to pay my mortgage. I hated that. It's so degrading for a man who had been successful and had paid 40% tax most of my working life. I suddenly became just another statistic of the unemployed.

After about four weeks, I was offered a job at the Job Centre. It paid absolute peanuts but I had to work. I had to do something. The house was up for sale, my youngest daughter, Sue, was being sent home from school in tears because of what had happened to her family. I was in such a state that one morning on my way to work, I was passing

All Saints Church. I stopped and went in. I sat at the back, looked up at the altar and said, "You Bas***D! What have I done to deserve this?" Needless to say, I didn't get an answer straight away.

Some weeks later, I was on a training course, learning how to deal with the poor unemployed people like I had been, only a short while before. At the other end on the table was a tall blonde lady with a lovely smile. She seemed to know what happened to a person and their benefits, when they had been divorced.

At the lunch break, I said to her, "Please don't think I'm being forward but, I'm about to go through a divorce myself and I don't know what I'm supposed to do". I must have had a 'lost puppy' sort of 'hang dog' look about me because we went and sat in the park to eat our sandwiches and just chatted. She told me later that she'd picked up a parking ticket because of our chat.

This, I firmly believe, was the answer to my question when I was in All Saints Church in Maidstone. To cut a long story short, we began a friendship that has lasted so well that, as I write this part of my story, we've been married for 20 years.

Basically she picked me up out of the gutter, said, You're quite a nice bloke. Dusted me off and I know I'll be forever grateful to her for saving me from myself. Maureen came into my life when I was 48 and alone with my daughter Sue at 15. She brought her son Adam, who was 14, six feet four, 15 stone with her and suddenly, I had a new family and a reason to believe. It needs to be said again that I will be forever grateful to my Maureen. She has given me a lot of love, understanding and support that I could never have dreamed possible. I can't be the easiest bloke to live with. She maintains that if there's anything that comes into my life that isn't music-related, I soon forget about it. I don't mean to be like that but I have a sort of "butterfly brain", you know, I flit from one thing to another in a matter of seconds. She introduced me to the Theatre in many types of performances, which I now absolutely love. I've "rubbed shoulders" with quite a few famous faces while at a show or a play. I'll get round to some of them soon.

Anyway, the best thing to come out of meeting Maureen was, after a couple of years together, WE GOT MARRIED! Adam, her son, gave her away, my daughters Jane, Karen and Sue were her bridesmaids and Roy, my son-in-law was my best man. That was one brilliant day. We were surrounded by friends and family, all having a great time. Thank you all.

After a couple of years, working as a Benefit Fraud Officer, I had a call from an old pal with whom I had worked at LWT, Tony Smith. He had been working at a Scandinavian TV Station called TV3 and he was about to leave. He said it was about time I got myself back into television and that I should apply for his old job. So I did, and I got it! I had done a few freelance jobs at a 'one horse' TV station called 'Superchannel' but it wasn't real television. They were only playing at it and their audience was teenagers, a couple of cats and a dog.

TV3 had channels in Sweden, Norway and Denmark. The transmission was done via satellite from the set-up at West Drayton, near Heathrow.

We had the most diverse selection of staff that you could ever imagine. From a few English and a few Scandies, plus a Canadian, a Portuguese, Irish, Welsh, Arab etc. We also had a couple of Gays who were excellent people! The young guy who worked in the video tape library, coined a phrase that I'll never forget. He said, "I'm not Gay, I'm simply of alternative sexuality!" That is sheer brilliance and

I admired him for it.

I had a good time working there and some of the Scandy female administration staff were the classic tall, blue-eyed, blondes that most red-blooded males lust after.

One of those, who was a department manager and about 26, came up to me at the coffee machine one morning and stood six inches from my nose and said, "Malcolm, you're the only man here, who is tall enough for me" There's no answer to that which sprang to mind instantly so, being a happily married man, I beat a hasty retreat!

There was one English girl who was beautiful and had a brilliant personality but she spoke like what is now called an Essex Girl.

At the staff Christmas party one year, the chief executive was on his feet, giving his 'thank you for your efforts in the past year' speech, when this girl walks up to him, a little the worse for wear, says, "That's enough of the Scandy B*****KS! Let's get on with some drinking!" You could have cut the air with a knife and then everyone dissolved into helpless laughter.

I became good friends with our American, Company Vice-

President, Dave Uhrich. We used to play golf together and we're still friends to this day, although he now lives back in the USA. We visit occasionally both ways.

After a while, TV3 was taken over by another company called DAL so, as usual, redundancies were on the cards. More so-called sophisticated equipment meant it needed less people to run it.

Just before redundancy candidates were selected, the guy who was to be the new head of transmission came to talk to all the transmission staff. We were all seated round a large table, waiting, when in "swans" this apparition in a top-of-the-range Armani suit, shoulder-length hair and an American style grin from ear to ear. He opened with,"Hey Guys! We've got some seriously sexy gear going in here!" We looked at each other in amazement. Electronic equipment, SEXY GEAR! Do me a favour. He'd come from SKY TV so that said it all. I was half hoping that I would be on the list to go. Well I was right. A third of us were ear marked for the tip. I'm not supposed to say this but I'm sure ageism came into it.

Anyway, at a time like this, you call everyone you know in the business and ask for a job. I was very fortunate to know quite a few, as I was now getting a bit long in the tooth for TV. I called a good friend, Janet Marbrook, who was a Vice President of a company called Flextech. They used the Pearson TV facilities in London to transmit minority channels like LIVING, BRAVO, CHALLENGE TV and TV TRAVELSHOP. Not necessarily the best programmes but I needed a job. These channels were totally computer-controlled so I had to learn to do my job all over again. It was tough for me because I had never had any proper training on computers. I managed to get by and ended up working on TV TRAVELSHOP where I could do less damage. I met up with an old LWT colleague, GLEN TOMSETT, who was an "in-vision Announcer" in those days. He worked there with his lady wife JUDY MADDOCKS. Nice people.

When I was out for a walk one lunchtime, I was in Goodge Street when I saw a familiar face talking with some people on the pavement. It was singer LEO SAYER. As I got closer, Leo grabbed my arm and said, "I'm sure this guy is more famous than me." "I don't think so Leo" Says I. Anyway, they were Americans and so I ended up having my photo taken with Leo and then with their "large" daughter and son. Then I went on my merry way.

Working at Pearson TV was very physically demanding for me. It was 12.5 hour shifts and my day started by catching the 6.09 am train to be in work by 7.30. This meant that I didn't get home until 8.50pm on average. At weekends, I had to drive, as there was always 'works' on the rail lines to be done. I got so tired that, in the space of three weeks, I managed to get nine points on my driving license. Two of three points for speeding over 50mph and one of three points for going into a yellow box when my exit wasn't clear. This job was wearing me out!

My years of experience didn't really matter any more. The job was different. It seemed like all that mattered was to get pictures and sound up on the screen. There was little camaraderie amongst the staff. Unlike the years at LWT, where we all used to work for and with each other and we had a sense of pride in our work.

I'll never forget one day, when I went to the Channel Manager and suggested that a member of staff from each section should be seconded to another department for a week or two, so that they could understand the problems and pitfalls of one another's section. That way it would help things to gel together and sort out some of the difficulties. "Good idea", she said. "Put it in an e-mail to me".

"Why?" said I. "I need it in writing", was her answer. Her secretary was sitting listening so I said,

"Can't she write it down?" "No, I want you to do it".

I didn't want any credit for the suggestion so I just said, "Forget it" and walked away. Sometimes common sense just doesn't apply no matter how you look at it in some people's eyes.

Eventually I began to fold up. My Doctor took me off work for a few weeks and after that had happened a couple of times I was sent to the company Doctor in Harley Street for a independent check up. I was kind of relieved when he said, "Malcolm, this job is not for you anymore".

His report back to management resulted in me being offered early retirement with a pay-off. I was only 62 but Maureen and I thought we could manage. I was receiving a couple of pensions from earlier jobs and I was still doing gigs here and there. That wasn't bringing in enough money to worry the taxman, so that's the way it went. I'd had a great career in television but I have to say I didn't miss it as a job, but I did miss the people that I worked with. I met a lot of great friends and I'm proud to say that I'm still in contact with an awful lot of them today.

Chapter 21   Other Brief "Shoulder Rubbing"

This business about "rubbing shoulders" has happened to me at many odd instances.

Take the time when I was at The Old Vic with my wife Maureen to see the production of *Amadeus*, starring David Suchet (Hercule Poirot to the uninitiated). We get to the interval and I'm off to get some refreshment. I push open the door leading from the circle out to the bar and nearly decapitate the great KEVIN SPACEY! He hadn't long become the Artistic Director of The Old Vic at the time and I'd nearly killed him, metaphorically speaking. After my profound apology and a lot of dusting him down, he continued on his merry way.

Another triple shoulder rubbing happened at another theatrical outing. We were sitting, once again, in the circle behind a face that I knew instantly. The lady beside me said, quite loudly, "Here, is that who I think it is?" I nodded and put my finger to my lips in a hushing fashion. He turned, smiled and said, "Good evening" to me. It was HRH Prince Michael out for an evening's entertainment and not wishing to be bothered by anyone. Rightly so.

When it came to the interval, I asked Maureen if she would like a drink. She said she'd prefer an ice cream. We were in the circle, the ice cream lady was in the stalls. Off I go and as soon as I began to cross through the circle bar, *BOOF!* Someone walked straight into me. "Oh, sorry pal", says this Scottish accent. I look up and it's only DAVID TENNANT (*Doctor Who* himself!). He's brushing me down and asking if I'm OK? "I'm fine", says I, "And you're obviously in a hurry to get somewhere. Can I get you a drink?", says David. "No thanks, says I, I'm really OK". So I continue on my way.

Half way down the stairs, I spot BILL BAILEY, that lunatic comedian and brilliant musician, coming up the other way. Now, I've never met Bill but I grab his hand and ask how he is. He tells me he's fine and asks if I'm enjoying the show. We exchange a few pleasantries and I go on my way.

I get to the bottom of the stairs and I spot the toilet door and think I'd better make use of the facilities before getting the ice creams.

The door is whipped open before I can grab the handle and there stands actor MARC WARREN (Danny Blue from the BBC show *HUSTLE*). He holds the door open for me and says, "After you, young man". Young Man! He's in his early 30s and I'm.......... twice his age. When I get back to my seat and tell Maureen of my encounters, she says, "It always happens to you, doesn't it! Where are they then?" And at that very moment, DAVID TENNANT walked across the front of the stalls, just in time for me to point him out.

David Tennant (Great)

One sunny summer morning, I was driving to the LWT Studios and I was waiting at the crossing right beside the stage door of The Old Vic near Waterloo. I look to my left and there, sitting on a bicycle in a beautiful suit and tie, is that great actor NIGEL HAWTHORN. I caught his eye and waved. He smiled, saluted me and said, "Isn't this fun!" and swept off down the road. I laughed my head off.

On another occasion, I was in heavy traffic in Knightsbridge. When a very powerful motorbike came out of a driveway beside me. On the bike was SIR RALPH RICHARDSON. In full, light grey leathers and a silver helmet. I let him in. He smiled, waved me a "Thank you" and roared off towards The Albert Hall. Impressive to say the least.

I got a call from my son's father-in-law Rob, asking if I would play in The Henry Cooper Pro Celebrity Golf Tournament at Nizels Golf Club in Tonbridge one day. They were hard up for celebrities and Rob had told them that he knew a bloke (Me!) who had appeared on radio/TV/and had a mention in the Guinness Book of Hit Singles (No.49). Naturally I accepted the invitation. In the changing room, I met several celebrities including ED

STEWART who I told that I had worked at LWT when he was doing his Stewpot Show and the incomparable JESS CONRAD once again. Jess introduced me to the whole room by saying, in a very loud voice, "This young man and I, have trodden the boards together back in the 60s".

Of course, I played like a complete turnip during the day but at dinner, I enjoyed myself immensely. There was a sports quiz after dinner. First we all had to stand up and when the question was asked, and you got it wrong you had to sit down. I got to the last two. A Lady member and me. Anyway I lost and afterwards I went over to "Our 'Enery" and said, Henry, you're a great bloke but your quizzes are crap!

Lucky for me, he roared with laughter and shook my hand 'til my knuckles cracked. He could easily have punched my lights out but he didn't thank goodness.

Maureen and I took a City Break holiday to Dublin and on our way there, we had the fresh-faced young guys from BOYZONE sitting in front and across the aisle from us. They were just about breaking big into the business but they hadn't let it go to their heads. They signed autographs for everyone who asked them.

Our 'Enery, One of the nicest guys ever!

I have to tell you the funny story of what happened at Dublin airport. You have to listen to the story inside your head with an Irish accent.

We arrived at the check-in desk and the guy said,

 Now, yer plane's gonna be a bit late so we've up-graded you to de earlier one. (What ?)

So we've got time for a drink before take-off. We go to the elliptical shaped bar and ordered a pint of Guinness for me, and a half for Maureen. As is the usual way, the barman pours half the glass and leaves it to settle. He goes off to serve another traveller and his pal the other barman comes around from the other side.

He says, Are yes alright der Sur?

I say, Yes thanks, and I understand that when God made time, he made plenty of it.

He looked at me with a glint in his eye and said,

Well he never worked in dis F***ing bar did he Sur?

Only an Irishman could get away with that. Brilliant!

Chapter 22   The Return Of The Packabeats!

In 2003, I was at the retirement party of Ian "Stoo" Stewart, the founder member and drummer "extraordinaire" of THE PACKABEATS, when he showed me a magazine called *THUNDERBOLT.*

This was the publication of The Joe Meek Appreciation Society. There was a picture of the band with all the wrong names under the wrong people. This sort of thing always incenses me, so I contacted the editor Mark Newson to remonstrate with him. He turned out to be such a nice bloke that I couldn't tell him off. He wanted to meet me and do an interview with Stoo and I for the magazine.

As you can see, I have a multitude of photos, articles, press cuttings etc. so we did.

The upshot of that, meant THE PACKABEATS reforming to play for the JMAS AGM the following April 4th 2004. It was held in a pub in Battersea. Not exactly The Palladium or The O2 Arena, but no more than we deserved after 43 years of not playing together. It was tremendous fun to do and although we were pretty rusty, the Meeksters seemed to like us.

On the back of that, another magazine called *PIPELINE*, asked us to play at their annual convention on Easter Sunday April 11th 2004.

That was a fairly "hairy" occasion, because we had to play all instrumentals and not sort of busk our way through Rock'n'Roll standards. That's what THE PACKABEATS were known as, an instrumental group. We made it OK anyway. On the bill at *PIPELINE* was one of THE SHADOWS many bass guitarists, ALAN JONES. A good player but I thought he looked more like a bank manager than a musician. Nice guy though.

With these bits and pieces going on, there was a renewed interest in THE PACKABEATS, so I cobbled together a CD of our old Joe Meek recordings along with some tracks recorded with TONY HOLLAND, plus some live tracks from *PIPELINE*. The old "Packafans" came out and bought them in their droves! Well a few hardliners bought them. Years ago, we'd sold 13,000 records and never received a penny for them, so we felt justified in earning a few quid after all this time.

Sanctuary Records, kept on issuing our Joe Meek records on their compilation CDs and still we got nothing!

The Packabeats at Pipeline Convention 2004

At one time, I counted 11 separate CDs, which had either PACKABEATS or Hi-Fi's recordings on them. Not fair really.

We were asked to go to a recording studio in Bath, called Western Star, to re-record two of our Joe Meek tunes. "The Traitors" and "Dream Lover". Now Alan Wilson of

Western Star, was never going to better Joe's "Traitors" but we leapt at the chance of re-recording "Dream Lover". We always hated what Joe had done to that one. Like the two keyboards, a quarter-tone out of tune!

Alan did a good job and it came out on his *Tribute To Joe Meek* album.

There was a play on in the West end of London called *TELSTAR*. Written by NICK MORAN and starring CON O'NEILL as Joe. I went to see it with a pal of mine, David Tinley. Who was very interested in getting THE PACKABEATS back into a studio to do some more recordings.

That play was brilliant! CON O'NEILL was perfect in the part of Joe Meek. When he first appeared, I had a look of sheer disbelief on my face. David and I went to the stage door afterwards to see if we could meet Con. We did meet him and NICK MORAN and I just had to tell them how good I thought it was. Nick asked me what was my involvement with Joe Meek and when I told him, he was really interested.

Then, right out of the blue, something amazing happened!

I received an e-mail asking if I knew THE PACKABEATS. I said I was a PACKABEAT. It turned out to be the Editor of a film company, who wanted to get permission to use our recording of "The Traitors" over the opening titles of a new film about the life and times of Joe Meek, called *TELSTAR*.

We had been awarded ownership of our own recordings and so it was all down to me to act for the band and agree the use of it, for the film.

Talk about fame after all those years!

CON O'NEILL was playing Joe again and PAM FERRIS, his ill-fated landlady, KEVIN SPACEY, his business partner, J.J.FIELD, JAMES CORDEN and RALF LITTLE played members of THE TORNADOS (who had the No. 1 hit with TELSTAR).

Before the film came out, THE PACKABEATS were asked to play at what was called A JOE MEEK FEST. We had never intended to play seriously again. Too much time had passed and I was really the only one who had continued to play. I had been with my function band HAPPY DAZE since November '79 and I was still doing it.

So I got the guys out again and we did a bit of rehearsing.

We only had to play five or six numbers, so it wouldn't be too difficult. We opened the show and as we were the only band to still have all the original members, we walked on to enthusiastic applause. Then I tripped over Ted Harvey's Bass lead! His bass crashed to the floor, I turned to the audience with arms open and palms upward in a "What?" fashion as if it was intentional and they all laughed and off we went. We got through our set and it was fine.

Next up was another of Joe Meek's bands THE SCORPIONS. They tore through their set in fine form. They were all good guys too.

Then it was the turn of THE HONEYCOMB. I say HONEYCOMB because there was only one of the originals there! That was MARTIN MURRAY, the rhythm guitarist. He was a bit of a star, but never mind. They also back another of Joe's singers, BOBBY RIO. He was a good old boy.

During the interval, we were all in the Green Room backstage having a cup of tea, when BRUCE WELCH from THE SHADOWS, came up to me and asked which band I was in. When I told him THE PACKABEATS, he said, "THE PACKABEATS! "THE TRAITORS"! What a great record! You could've been us you know". I said, Bruce, "I think you'll find that your singer was a bit better than ours" (No offence TONY).

CLEM CATTINI'S TORNADOS opened the second half. He's the only one still there. HEINZ is dead, so is ALAN CADDY. ROGER LAVERNE was living in Mexico and he hadn't been too well lately and GEORGE BELLAMY lives somewhere in Spain I believe. George's son Matt, plays with the band called MUSE. He must be very proud of his boy. While THE TORNADOS were playing, I was talking with CLIFF BENNETT, when suddenly he heard an announcement down on the stage. He said, "I hope that's not me?" Then an intro started up and it was! He was off down the stairs like a steam train and just made it to the stage for his first number, "Slow Down". How appropriate!

CRAIG DOUGLAS was guest artist on the show and he arrived with a walking stick. We were all wondering what was wrong, when he told us that he'd had a hernia operation recently and he was struggling a bit. However he did his spot like a true professional. He made everyone see the funny side of a man in his late 60s singing "Teenager In Love".

Bruce Welch at the Meekfest Show

Top of the bill, rightly so, was JOHN LEYTON. He was never really a singer, more of an actor but he always gave a good account of himself and today was no exception. He had the audience with him right from the start and when he did his famous hit Johnny Remember me, he had a gorgeous soprano by the name of SUZI JARI to hit the high notes that featured on the original recording. She hit the high notes with all the guys on the show for all the obvious reasons!

Somebody told my local newspaper, *The Kent and Sussex Courier* about my involvement in the film and they came round to interview me for a front-page article. BBC TV Newsroom Southeast saw that and I was interviewed for the News show by the stunning RITA CHACRABATI (what a beautiful girl). I even got to do a BBC Radio Kent Drive Time interview, which was heard by that great DJ from the days of the pirate ships and BBC radio, ROGER "TWIGGY" DAY.

He asked me to come on his Radio Kent Show to talk about the film. Well I was booked to do about ten minutes but ended up being there for nearly an hour! We had such a laugh, recounting stories of what went on in the 60s and some of the places where we played and what went on. Roger is a really nice guy and long may he continue.

On the back of the publicity, I had a visit from the local tax office would you believe! I came back from walking my dog and there was a buff envelope containing a letter telling me that they needed to "discuss my Tax situation". WHAT!!!!! I phoned them and they wanted to know where

Malcolm Lenny

I'd been. (Out with my dog).

The local *Courier* Newspaper headline had said,

BAND ROCKS ON AS FILM CASH ROLLS IN AFTER 50 YEARS.

NO! Wrong on all counts! I had to explain that we'd been paid a modest figure for the rights to the film and that wasn't going to solve the National Debt problem. Then it was, What about all these gigs with the PACKABEATS? What, THREE GIGS! Do me a favour. Then it was, What about all these gigs with HAPPY DAZE? I explained that it was an occasional band that played mostly for fun. I ended up saying that I'd paid 40% tax most of my working life and if any unexpected funds came my way, I would contact the Tax Office and ask for a Tax Return Form. Needless to say, nothing further has happened in either direction. When the film was ready to be released, they did a "Cast & Crew" showing at The Empire Leicester Square. Maureen came with me and so did The PACKABEATS Organist Derrick Leach and his wife Jenny. We stood talking outside with CLEM CATTINI of The TORNADOS, and his wife. What a lovely "Geezer" Clem is. He said, "I might not be able to see the whole film through". "Why's that?", says I. "I'm playing in Amsterdam tonight!" Then we took our seats for the showing.

When that film started and up came the PACKABEATS recording of "THE TRAITORS" over the opening credits, my heart was in my mouth! Maureen squeezed my arm so hard that she nearly broke the skin! Proud or what!

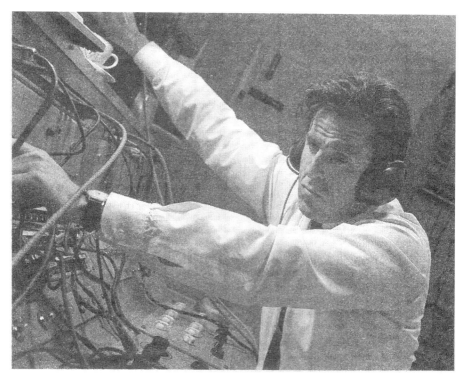

Con O'Neill as Joe Meek in the film Telstar

It was a great film. CON O'NEILL was brilliant again as JOE MEEK and apart from a little bit of poetic licence with the script, it was pretty much true to the story.

After the film, we visited the bar for a bit of socialising. I congratulated Con on his performance. He asked me what was my involvement in the film and I told him that I was the Lead Guitarist on the opening credits. He said, "What a great piece of music! Well done".

I told the actor NIGEL HARMAN who played JESS CONRAD that he was so like Jess in those days, even to look at. I explained that I had backed Jess on a few shows back in the 60s. The sort of "fight" between Jess and Heinz actually did happen but it was a bit like "Balloons on sticks at ten paces, no hitting in the face!" Those two guys were always trying to get more girls screaming at them than the other.

I then met the Director NICK MORAN again and he introduced me to SIMON JORDAN who had put the money up to make the film He was the main shareholder in Crystal Palace Football Club at the time. I asked him how he managed to get involved in *TELSTAR* and his answer was, I thought, should I buy another couple of players or do something a bit more permanent? I'm very glad he did because now we have a record of the life of one of the innovators of British pop music, whose genius will be remembered for a long time to come.

Nick Moran, actor and co-writer of the film Telstar"

I just thought I'd mention that I got The PACKABEATS to record a final album of instrumentals, just to prove we

273

could still play a bit.I called it *This Is It!* (long before Michael Jackson stole the title!) because there wouldn't be any more. I was right because dear old Derrick died in 2016.

The Packabeats last & final recording

How about a few more Shoulders?

I was booked to play with HAPPY DAZE at the wedding of the daughter of a friend near Croydon in Surrey The Bride's father had seen a few weddings falter, when it came to inexperienced family members giving speeches, so he booked TOM O'CONNOR to masquerade as a member of the family. The father introduced "Uncle Tom from Liverpool" and Tom went into his speech. He was hilarious! He must have done half an hour and at the end, we all were exhausted from laughing.

I spoke briefly to Tom before we played and told him that I'd met him once before at an ITV Natural Break Golfing Event at Royal Lytham and St Anne's a while back. I told him that there he told one of the funniest jokes I had ever heard. He asked me to tell it to him. It went like this:-

(In a Liverpool accent) I pulled into the car park at a local Liverpool Golf Club and as I got out, a Snotty-nosed little kid said, "Look after yer car Mister?" I said, "Look in the back son. What do you see there? It's a dog. Yes, it's not just an ordinary dog. It's a Rottweiller. With him in the back, I don't need a snotty-nosed kid to look after it!" The kid said, "Puts out fires does he?" Brilliant!

275

Tom even laughed at my Liverpool accent. I introduced him to my wife Maureen and they had a nice little chat. When he left, he kissed her on the cheek and said goodbye. It made her day. Tom O'Connor, you are a lovely man!

In 2010 Maureen and I went on a P & O cruise to the Baltics on board their new ship *The Ventura*. It was a monster! I felt that it was a bit like a floating Milton Keynes and we wouldn't encounter the same people on consecutive days.Anyway, on those kind of ships there's always a multitude of entertainment going on. There was a talk by Margaret Thatcher's daughter CAROL THATCHER, who needed and interpreter. She was so incoherent in her speaking we thought perhaps that she had used a bit too much "lubrication" for her vocal chords. We left after ten minutes.

In one of the evening entertainment bars, was singer PAUL DAVINCI. Now for those not in the know so to speak, it was Paul Davinci who sang the lead vocal for THE RUBETTES on their massive hit "Sugar Baby Love". I had a chat with Paul after his first set and I told him that I thought he never really got the recognition that he deserved for that record. He told me he wasn't paid much for it either! He had developed into a first rate entertainer and he even sang a mainstream almost jazz version of "Sugar Baby Love" without the high falsetto voice. He was really very good.

Some of the other musical entertainment was a bit suspect. There was a Rolling Stones Tribute (I hate that word Tribute!) Band without a bass player, would you believe! Naff or what?The Jazz Trio in the late night bar was odd to say the least. Piano, Bass and Drums. The piano player sang, well I say "sang" but when requested to sing "That's Why The Lady Is A Tramp" it became obvious that he had no idea how the middle eight went! It went any which way but right. Maureen asked the drummer if he could sing because the piano player can't! Bless her. She always tells it like it is.

There was a four piece Motown-style vocal group who were very good singers and movers but they sang to backing tapes. Shame. The next morning they were having breakfast at the same time as us and I asked, Why backing tapes? I was told that P & O won't pay for their usual six piece band. That's the old story of "spoiling the ship for a 'hap'eth of tar" I think.

277

There was also a woman doing a talk on Life Coaching. I saw her picture in the ship's itinerary and I thought I recognised her face. I was right, it turned out to be AnnA Rushton who had sat alongside me in the Transmission suite at London Weekend Television all those years ago.Maureen and I went to see AnnA (that is how she spells her name) and she was shocked and as pleased as I was to see her again. We enjoyed a couple of meals all together during the cruise.AnnA was very helpful in making me finish this book.

A few months ago, a friend of mine by the name of Henry Barnes who is a guitar teacher, session musician and also plays in a couple of really good bands, phoned me to tell me a little story, as he called it.

He's was working in the "pit band" for the show in the West End of London called *THE JERSEY BOYS*. I've seen it a couple of times and it's just brilliant. It's the story of The Four Seasons (featuring the "sound of Frankie Valli"). I always loved their music and I've sung the Frankie Valli part, but that was a long time ago when I had a good falsetto range.

Anyway, that's not the story. Henry said that he'd got hold

of a ticket to see Eric Clapton and Steve Winwood at The
Albert Hall. He also had a back-stage pass. So after the
show he went back to see if he could speak to Eric. It
turned out that Eric was surrounded by people, so Henry
couldn't get close. However, Steve Winwood had a break
in chatting with fans so Henry steamed in. In their
conversation, Steve asked Henry if he had seen the new
film about Joe Meek. Henry answered that he hadn't but a
friend's band had played over the opening titles."Who was
that?" Asked Steve. "The PACKABEATS", replied Henry."I
know The PACKABEATS," said Steve. "They made some
good records". Wow! Steve Winwood knows The
PACKABEATS! We must've been better than I thought!

I think I mentioned that, since I retired, I do a bit of part-
time work, for fun, in my local music shop in Tonbridge,
Kent, The American Guitar Centre.I was in there recently
when a guy came in and asked if we hire out PA systems.I
told him that we don't hire out equipment. Anyway we
were having a nice old chat about music when in came his
friend who was a genuine Native American Indian. He was
a musician as well so it went from this to that and then
another guy who works in the shop said, "Why don't you
hire them your PA for tonight and make yourself a few

quid."

So that's what we arranged to do.

Later that evening, they turned up at my house to collect the gear. A lady, who was dressed in hippy-type clothes got out of their car and introduced herself to me. Would you believe that she was MELANIE, the lady who had a Worldwide hit with the song "Brand New Key"! You know the song, it goes,"Now I've got a brand new pair of roller skates, you've got a brand new key" etc. She came to thank me for the use of my PA. We started talking on my driveway when she said, "This is a really nice garden." I said, "This is all my wife's doing. She's good at gardening". Out came Maureen, I introduced her to Melanie and they went into the house while we men loaded up the gear. Next minute they came back out and Melanie had her arms full of flowers from our garden. She was such a nice, warm person.

We were on holiday in Vienna, Austria in 2013 when a guy in the tour party started talking about himself and his Hofner President Guitar and what he did and used to do with it. I kept a bit quiet about my own involvement in music throughout the years. That was until I started to

Melanie, the "Brand New Key" Girl

think to myself, This guy likes to be the Life-& Soul of the party. So I casually mentioned that I had a few guitars. Then he asked how long I had played and I told him. "Who did you play with?" Was his next question. When I mentioned the dear old PACKABEATS, he said, "I remember them! My band used to play some of their records! They were really good!"

Then I talked a bit about The Hi-Fi's and all the bits and pieces that I did with them. Then I told him about our last two trips back to Germany with the surviving members of The Hi-Fi's in 2012/13 and how well we had gone down with our old "fans" from way back in '65-'67. After that, he went a bit quiet about himself.

It's funny but I never realised that I had actually played a small part in the British music scene and I'm really proud of that.

Do you remember, Dear reader, how I said that I rubbed shoulders with a few more people at the theatre? Well the last one was when Maureen and I went to see *A Chorus Line* at the Palladium in London. We sat right behind Nigel Planer that tremendous actor who came to fame as Neil the Hippie in the TV show *The Young Ones*.

The first time I went to the Palladium was in the late '60s. I went to see *La Cage aux Folles* (The Birdcage) and sitting right behind me were ARTHUR NEGUS from a TV Antique show and actor VICTOR SPINETTI (the Mad Jaffa

Cake Eater). Mr. Spinetti has done far more and better things than that commercial in his lifetime I know. The Beatles film *Help!* for instance.

Recently I was up in the Charing Cross Road in London's West End. I was helping to make a documentary about "My First Guitars" for the magazine called *PIPELINE*. When I had finish my bits "to Camera", I almost walked into the actor and comedian BRADLEY WALSH. I only mention that because it points out the fact that anybody can rub shoulders with the famous if you just keep your eyes open and your wits about you.

Recently, Maureen and I went on a short break to Portsmouth to see The *Mary Rose.* Absolutely fantastic! We had one of the original team of divers to talk to us before and afterwards. He was CHRIS DOBBS. He was a lovely guy and spellbinding in his enthusiasm for the whole project from discovery to displaying the ship. We bought him a drink back at the hotel and had an hour or so of personal chat. Then a few months later, there was a T.V. documentary on The *Mary Rose* and there was CHRIS DOBBS. Just as we had met him at Portsmouth.

These little "bits & pieces" of fame still keep coming out of the woodwork. A German guy called Bernhard Budts contacted me to say that he was writing a book called *Geboren 1950* (Born 1950) about the music scene in Monchengladbach from the 50s and through the 60s. Of course the good old Hi-Fi's had to be part of that didn't we? So I wrote him a bit about the great times we had there and gave him a few pictures. It's a full size hardback book with loads of good stuff in it, but you have to be able to read German!

Then I got an e-mail from a guy called Tom Lee who was compiling a website about steamship ferries. This is a really interesting website. So out came my anecdotes about The Hi-Fi's once again and our summer season on board *La Duchesse de Normandie* from Jersey.

Next was an American guy called Howard Massey, who was compiling a book called *The Great British Recording Studios*. He wanted some info on Joe Meek's studio at 304, Holloway Road, London. I was only too pleased to be asked to contribute. That is a great book! Loads of pictures of stars, big & small and terrific technical information too for the enthusiasts.

Then it was a mail from an Australian guy by the name of

Mark Tinson. He's quite a big name "down under". Again it was my connection with Joe Meek and THE PACKABEATS. He wanted a Meek artist and apparently I'm one of the few left still gigging. He liked what I'd played on our record "The Traitors" back in '63. He asked me if I'd play, as a Guest Artist, an instrumental track on his next album of Surf Tunes. In this modern day of the Internet, I was able to record my Lead Guitar part here in England on a WAV file (?) and send it to him via the ether. Ah, isn't technology a wonderful thing? But so were my early recordings with Joe Meek in his little flat in amongst all the screens and mattresses with all the cables leading out through the door from one room to another. It's all very different nowadays.

A couple of years ago, I decided to draw HAPPY DAZE to a natural end. Well, it was getting hard to find good gigs and the travelling was getting too much. One of the main problems is that functions and clubs seem to think it's better to book someone who stands up in front of pre-recorded backing tracks and just sing, or pretend to be playing a guitar. What gets me is when people say, Isn't he good!

Well no he isn't! It's only like Karaoke really but some of them claim to be a "tribute act". It's just a con and it's doing real musicians out of work.

I've been doing some gigs here & there for the last few years in a duo called Rich Picture with a good mate name of Mick Abbott. He plays Bass, I play Guitar, we use an electronic drum machine and we both sing. Nothing too serious or too regular, just good 50s & 60s music.

Anyway, a nice local guy name of Tony Green asked me to join him and play some Country songs just for fun. So I did. Cutting a long story short again, Tony & I recruited my old pal Pete Mills, from my skiffle group days when we were 15, on Bass guitar and then his Grandson Sam Baldock came in on 2nd guitar, keyboards, banjo, mandolin etc etc etc. We're having a great time playing 50s 60s 70s 80s Pop songs, Rock'n'Roll and Country, in local pubs & clubs for peanuts. We're not out to make money, just to have a good time. We've recorded three CDs, two straight from our usual sets and the third one is 16 Christmas songs and 'though I say it myself, they're all pretty good! This band called Side by Side will see my time out 'til I join my old departed friends in that great gig in the sky.

Side by Side 2016.
L/R Sam Baldock, Tony Green, Me, Pete Mills in front

I've recently joined that fine bunch of chaps known as The Triumphs, who specialize in the music of Joe Meek. I'm on lead guitar and vocals again. We played at the anniversary show remembering 50 years since Joe died. We played a lot of obscure songs from Joe's artists of the time and provided backing for a couple too. Unfortunately there aren't very many of Joe's oringinal artists left these days. Still, we must strive to keep this music alive for as long as we can.

287

The Triumphs –
l-r Trevor Faul, Ken Penrose, Malcolm Lenny, Rob Bradford, Ray
Liffen

I've been a very fortunate man throughout my life, to have been able to do so many different things and to go to so many interesting places. It's mostly due to my involvement in music and of course working in Television has been a great help too. In this day and age of "The Selfie", I'm sorry but I don't have any of those. The memories are all inside my own head.

I hope you, dear reader, have enjoyed my story. Thank you.

Malcolm Lenny (Of no fixed percentage!)

Epilogue

This may sound a wee bit pretentious but this rubbing shoulders bit has gone on all through my life really. I find myself reading a newspaper or magazine or watching a film and I find myself saying, I met that person.

I like to think that I have been an extremely fortunate man to have been able to lead such a full and varied life and for that I am very grateful. Who knows, I might even live long enough to get my telegram from Her Majesty Queen Elizabeth II. Although thinking rationally it'll probably be King William by then!

As a final postscript to this I would like to say that I've taken a few risks career-wise throughout my life and luckily most of them have paid off. So if you young people get to a crossroad in your life and you don't know what to do, I'll tell you. GO FOR IT! Otherwise you might find yourself regretting the fact that you didn't take the chance when you had it. Think about it, you're not all going to be professional footballers, pop singers or Television presenters but there might be a chance to do something different. So take it! You're only here once, life is not a rehearsal and it's not a video that you can rewind and do again.

Good Luck!

+++

If you have enjoyed this book please consider leaving a review online,

If you want further details of Silver Tabbies Publications featuring Music and Nostalgia – or even want your own life story - published drop us a line:

 silvertabbies+info@gmail.com

Front cover picture taken in Monchengladbach 1966 with The Hi-Fi's.

Back cover picture taken in Norway 2016 on a cruise with Maureen.

Printed in Great Britain
by Amazon